W9-AHO-011

Three Plays

Oklahoma Stories & Storytellers

Teresa Miller, Series Editor

Also by N. Scott Momaday

The Journey of Tai-me (Santa Barbara, 1967)

House Made of Dawn (New York, 1968, 1989)

The Way to Rainy Mountain (Albuquerque, 1969, 1976)

Angle of Geese and Other Poems (Boston, 1974)

Before an Old Painting of the Crucifixion, Carmel Mission, June, 1960
    (San Francisco, 1975)

The Gourd Dancer (New York, 1976)

Names: A Memoir (New York, 1976; Tucson, 1996)

The Ancient Child (New York, 1989, 1990)

In the Presence of the Sun: Stories and Poems, 1961–1991
    (New York, 1992)

Circle of Wonder: A Native American Christmas Story
    (Santa Fe, 1994; Albuquerque, 1999)

The Man Made of Words: Essays, Stories, Passages (New York, 1997)

In the Bear's House (New York, 1999)

Four Arrows and Magpie (Tulsa, 2006)

THREE PLAYS

The Indolent Boys
Children of the Sun
The Moon in Two Windows

N. SCOTT MOMADAY

UNIVERSITY OF OKLAHOMA PRESS : NORMAN

Library of Congress Cataloging-in-Publication Data
Momaday, N. Scott, 1934–
[Plays. Selections]
Three plays / N. Scott Momaday.
p. cm.
ISBN 978-0-8061-3828-2 (alk. paper)
1. Indians of North America—Drama. 2. Indian children—Drama.
3. Kiowa Indians—Drama. 4. Off-reservation boarding schools—
Drama. I. Title.
PS3563.047T48 2007
812'.54—dc22
2007003914

Three Plays: The Indolent Boys, Children of the Sun, and The Moon in Two
Windows is Volume 3 in the Oklahoma Stories & Storytellers series.

The paper in this book meets the guidelines for permanence and
durability of the Committee on Production Guidelines for Book
Longevity of the Council on Library Resources, Inc. ∞

Copyright © 2007 by N. Scott Momaday. Published by the University
of Oklahoma Press, Norman, Publishing Division of the University.
All rights reserved. Manufactured in the U.S.A.

1 2 3 4 5 6 7 8 9 10

CONTENTS

PREFACE

We have a man in the light of a fire, with trees in the background. Before him, on the ground, are seated men, women, and children. All eyes are upon the man, whose face is resilient in the ripples of light. His presence is profound. He wields an ancient power, the power of words. He is the storyteller, the worker of wonder. He plays upon the instrument of the human voice. It is a unique performance.

The telling of a story and the enactment of a play are closely related, for both are examples of oral tradition. Their vitality is that of the spoken word. Every telling of a story, every performance of a play is a unique happening. Something will inevitably change each time the story is told—the interpretation of the storyteller or the actor, the composition of the audience, the inflection of a word or a passage.

I came quite honestly to the writing of plays. I began my writing career as a poet, and a poet I remain. I believe that poetry is the highest expression of language. Poetry is meant to be heard. Stories and plays are meant to be heard. Without the element of sound, the instrument of the voice, their power and beauty are diminished. It is one thing to experience *Beowulf* on the printed page, quite another to hear it read, or better, to hear it recited from memory, as it was originally. The same may be said of the Book of Job or of *Hamlet*. These are poems in form and oral tradition in spirit. They have their best and fullest existence apart from writing. It is no accident that the greatest writer in English was a playwright. Shakespeare's language is the language of speech, the soul's breath. In our time and place, as in his, the play is the supreme vehicle of oral tradition.

The oral tradition of the American Indian is venerable and highly developed. For much of my life I have been a student and teacher of that tradition. The three plays in this collection issue from an indigenous continuum of thousands of years, an investment in language and literature that bespeaks the deepest workings of the human mind and heart.

There is an American Indian saying: In the beginning was the word, and it was spoken.

N. Scott Momaday

New Mexico and Oklahoma, 2006

ACKNOWLEDGMENTS

The process of play writing and performance is circular, and I am indebted to the following people for inspiration and support in the conception, writing, and performance of these plays.

Tazewell Thompson directed the world premiere of *The Indolent Boys* at the Syracuse Stage in Syracuse, New York. Michael Horse, artist and actor, was a vital part of the Santa Fe, New Mexico, production of *The Indolent Boys*, and of the Wells Fargo Radio Theatre version recorded at the Autry Center in Los Angeles.

Meir Ribalow directed *Children of the Sun* for its first performance at the Kennedy Center, Washington, D.C. Tazewell Thompson also assisted me in the initial transfer of *Children* from Kiowa creation myth to the stage. Dr. James and Judy Moore brought *Children of the Sun* to the Barter Theatre, the State Theatre of Virginia, where the Barter Theatre Company brought the play to magical life.

Beau and Jeff Bridges, who for years have been interested in and dedicated to the telling of the Carlisle story, contributed in a thousand ways to the creation of *The Moon in Two Windows*. Barbara Landis shared her considerable knowledge of the Carlisle story and made available to me indispensable documents and photographs. Not least, she arranged for me to stay in Jim Thorpe's old room at Carlisle while I was researching the play. Chris Eyre provided excellent advice and encouragement along the way.

For the many decisions that lead to the successful transfer of a play to the printed page, I am indebted to my friend and editor Teresa Miller; Steven Baker, managing editor at OU Press; and copyeditor Patricia Heinicke, Jr. Robert Schwartz of the Cumberland County Historical Society came up with just the right photographs for *The Moon in Two Windows*.

My dear friend and inspiration Bernard Pomerance taught me much of what I know about the art of the playwright. Finally, my wife, Barbara, was, and is, my muse.

The Indolent Boys

Kiowa Boarding School, Anadarko, Oklahoma. Courtesy of Patricia E. Henry, Mohawk Lodge Indian Store, Clinton, Oklahoma.

To those whose stories have fallen beyond reach

ABOUT THE PLAY

The Indolent Boys is based upon a tragedy that is now more than one hundred years old. In 1891 three young boys ran away from the Kiowa Indian Boarding School at Anadarko, Oklahoma, then Indian Territory, after the eldest boy had been whipped by a teacher for fighting. They headed for the camps where their families lived, some forty miles away. Overtaken by a terrible storm, they froze to death. Their frozen bodies were found by their relatives on a small bluff south of present-day Carnegie, Oklahoma. They were buried in the Indian way, simply and without ceremony.

The Kiowas, when they discovered the bodies, were enraged and grief-stricken. To signify their sorrow, the people cut off their hair or parts of their fingers or otherwise scarified themselves. They marched upon the school, beat up the superintendent, and threatened war. The teacher and "disciplinarian" who administered the whipping hid in the rafters of the school and then disappeared. Mother Goodeye, an aged Kiowa woman with one eye, searched for him. Armed with a knife, she meant to kill him. Although the Kiowas were deeply grieved and angry, a mortal confrontation was averted. The incident of "the frozen boys" is marked in the pictographic calendars of the Kiowas, and it remains fixed in their cultural memory.

The Kiowa Boarding School was one in a nationwide network of Indian schools based upon the ideas and methods of Richard Henry Pratt. In 1875 seventy-two warriors were taken prisoner after the Red River War, and Pratt conducted them to Fort Marion, Florida, for the purpose of "civilizing" them. Pratt also founded the prototypal Carlisle Indian School in Pennsylvania in 1879. His magnificent obsession was to convert Indians into white men, and his motto was "Kill the Indian and save the man."

I have heard the story of the boys who froze to death from the time I was a child. It is deeply and ever more dimly embedded in Kiowa oral tradition. After thinking of the boys for many years I determined to commemorate them in a play. I was greatly aided in the process by my Kiowa kinsmen, by others who knew of the story, and by the staff of the Oklahoma Historical Society and of the National Archives. In some sense the Kiowa boys, who in the ordinary currents of time would be nameless, have now become visible in the long lens of history. When I think of this phenomenon I think also of the numberless souls whose stories have fallen beyond reach. To all of those, unknown, I dedicate this play.

PERFORMANCE HISTORY

The Indolent Boys received its first public performance in a staged reading on February 7 and 8, 1992, at the Agassiz Theatre at Harvard University. Presented by the Harvard Native American Program, the reading was directed by Gitta Honegger and featured Edna Manitowabi as Mother Goodeye, Clapham Murray as G. P. Gregory, Ken Cheeseman as Barton Wherritt, Patricia Randell as Carrie, Dwayne (Little Deer) Manitowabi as John Pai, N. Scott Momaday as Emdotah, and Manasseh Begay and Forrest Cross as Kiowa schoolboys.

The play had its world premiere on February 8, 1994, at the Syracuse Stage, Syracuse, New York. Tazewell Thompson directed, and Terry Tsotigh created the music for this production. Terry Tsotigh portrayed the role of a musician; Ching Valdes/Aran, the part of Mother Goodeye; Robert Hogan, G. P. Gregory; Kelly Morgan, Barton Wherritt; Jonathan Fisher, John Pai; Twyla Hafermann, Carrie; and Gordon Tootoosis, Emdotah.

In 2005 a radio adaptation of *The Indolent Boys* written by Lori Tubert was broadcast on the AIROS (American Indian Radio on Satellite) network. The Wells Fargo Radio Theatre program and the Autry Museum of Western Heritage cooperated with AIROS in this production, which included a special introduction by the playwright.

CHARACTERS

MOTHER GOODEYE, an old Kiowa woman

G. P. GREGORY, the school superintendent

BARTON WHERRITT, a teacher

CARRIE, a teacher

JOHN PAI, a Kiowa schoolboy

EMDOTAH, a Kiowa man

SCHOOLCHILDREN

They are homesick,
they are going to the camps, they are camping.

> —In Kiowa oral tradition it is not unusual
> to speak of the dead in the present tense.

Akeah-de. They were camping.
What happened then was a wonderful
thing. It seemed that everything had to
do with wonder.

> —Huan-toa

PROLOGUE

The wheel in dim light. Indian flute and muted, unintelligible voices. Spotlight up stage left. Mother Goodeye stands hunched over a walking stick, twisted like herself. She is dressed in the manner of a Kiowa matron of the camps, in skins or trade cloth and moccasins, an apronlike sash, a simple shawl. She has but one eye. Her head hangs upon narrow, stooped shoulders, and she is humpbacked. She stands very still, except that her head and hands wobble just perceptibly with age. She seems quite frail, indeed feeble. But her good eye is bright and piercing, and when she speaks it becomes obvious at once that she is possessed of a remarkable vitality and presence of mind. Flute and voices fade. After a long moment she begins to speak, slowly at first, in a kind of rote recitation to herself.

MOTHER GOODEYE

> They are homesick,
> they are going to the camps,
> they are camping.

There is a pause in which she gathers herself up, and she speaks then conversationally to the audience, with animation.

> Oh, the little one, Mosatse! So bright-eyed, so playful! Big head, big stomach, like a baby! Ten years old. Mosatse. Eh, *neh, neh.* It's a funny name, isn't it—Mosatse? Say it, why don't you? MO SAT SE.

She beckons to the audience; it speaks the name.

> Yes, MO SAT SE. Yes, that's right. It's a funny name. It's a name like laughter. Well, his father was stolen, you see. A Mexicano, a Mexican man. Oh, those are brave, strong people, those Mexicanos. They fight like hell! And, goddam, they are hard to kill! Therefore, we *Gaigwu,* we Kiowas like to steal them. They are good for us, you see, like the corn and melons we steal from the Wichitas and the Osages, like the horses we steal from— from everybody. We are the best goddam horse thieves in the world.

Gleefully she shuffles, dances, once around her walking stick, waving her free
hand above her head and intoning at a high pitch, "Whoo, whoo! Whoo,
whoo! Eh neh neh neh!" She stops and catches her breath.

But that is another story. I tell it to you sometime. Well, when
this man was stolen he spoke his name, MOO SAT SO, no,
MOO SA CHO, no, MOO CHA CHO. But we *Gaigwu* cannot
make this name so well on our *Gaigwu* tongues, and so we call
the little one Mosatse. Anyway, you see, Mosatse is a nicer
name than MOO CA CHO, I think. And nicer than Jack, how he
is called at the Kiowa Boarding School. Jack! It's like a tree
cracking, or someone trotting on old, crusty snow. It's not a
name, it's a cough. *(pause)*

Then Koi-khan-hodle, twelve years old. He is homesick, he
is going to the camps, he is camping. Koi-khan-hodle. It means
—how do you call it?—"Dragonfly." At the Kiowa Boarding
School he is called Arrrrsh, Arsh . . . well, Arch. He is good with
horses, that one. What kind of a name is Arsh? Surely, surely it is
not the name of a young man who is good with horses. Koi-
khan-hodle, *that* is a name, a pretty damn good name, like a
shield. You know what is a shield?—a warrior's shield? Yes?
Dragonfly the warrior, the hunter, the horseman. Yes, you see. A
young man with a name like that will have a famous shield, you
see, and he will paint his horse in a certain way, and he will not
tell lies, and he will be a warrior, maybe a dog soldier, maybe a
Kaitsenko warrior. Koi-khan-hodle! Mosatse! Oh, the two of
them, the two little boys! *(pause)*

Then Seta, fifteen years old, called Sailor at the Kiowa
Boarding School. Like Koi-khan-hodle, neither a baby. Neither
a child nor a man—but somehow, it is a strange thing, an old
man. Think of it! Fifteen years old and an old man! It is a holy
thing, you see. An original boy, a boy priest, perhaps too a
warrior, a dog soldier like his namesake Set-angia, Sitting
Bear. Brave. Brave beyond belief. Brave to madness. And like
Set-angia he has white hair! Imagine! Fifteen years old, and he
has white hair. Oh, and he has a hole in his head, here. Even
Set-angia had no hole in his head—but only the one eye, like
me. *Eh neh neh neh.* I never thought of that! Seta and Set-angia,

and I. We have holes in our heads, you see. Surely that is a great sign and a powerful medicine. And Seta talks like an old man, foolish and wise like Saynday, like a medicine man. Oh, my boy! My original boy. (*pause*)

Mr. Wherritt whipped him, you see. Barton Wherritt whipped him with a leather strap. What kind of a name is Barton Wherritt? It is not the name of someone who is good with horses. It is not the name of someone who carries a famous shield. Barton, bear spittle, maybe, bear vomit. A Wherritt is a little, ugly, stinking bird, I think. And it makes a sound like a leather strap striking the back of a boy. The sound, oh, that was the terrible thing. The sound was flat and loud, like a tree splitting—BLACK! BLACK! BLACK! It was like that. It was a shameful thing, you see.

Blackout.

ACT ONE

Scene One

January 8, 1891, evening

The barely visible wheel is suspended in the blackness of the stage. Spotlight up on stage right. Two schoolchildren sit in desks. They appear to talk to themselves and each other, but we do not hear them. Lights up on center stage. Wherritt sits at teacher's desk on which are books, inkwell, bell, etc. An oil lamp gives a yellow tinge to his face. He is visibly agitated, on edge. He writes, mumbling to himself. He is dressed in a plain, rumpled suit and tie. Over his shoulder is the wheel, drawn on a hide. It is tacked to the wall or something like a bulletin board. Children's drawings of various objects or scenes are pinned around it. Its size and definition draw attention. Gregory enters stage left from the cold, removes cap and scarf, rubs hands vigorously. With the open door there are brief notes of flute and boys' voices echoing. The schoolchildren turn and stare intently. Gregory is older than Wherritt, more fastidious in his dress, and is jovial and officious at the same time. He has a favorable impression of himself. Wherritt is somewhat startled, somewhat irritated by the sudden intrusion.

GREGORY

> Lord, it is cold. I ask you, has it ever been so cold—here, I mean—since you came, Barton? Oh, good evening, good evening to you Barton.

WHERRITT

> Evening. No, not so cold as this.

GREGORY

> No. I thought not. Not nearly. But by God it happens, you know. It's the plains.

WHERRITT

> What? Excuse me, what?

GREGORY

> I said it's the plains, the Great Plains of the North American

Continent. There's no resistance, you know, no windbreak. The weather comes down from the north, the far north, unimpeded, un-im-peded, a thousand miles, gathering force the whole blasted way. Lord almighty!

WHERRITT

Yes, indeed, Lord almighty.

Gregory suddenly notices the wheel. Studies it for a moment over Wherritt's shoulder.

GREGORY

What in the world is that?

Wherritt turns and regards the wheel as well.

WHERRITT

It is . . . it is a drawing, an image drawn upon the skin of an animal, a Kiowa drawing, a pagan thing.

GREGORY

Yes, yes, I can see that it's a drawing. What is it a drawing of, may I ask?

He goes to the drawing, traces the wheel with his fingers.

WHERRITT

Well, I don't know. I believe that it's some sort of religious figure. I'm told it's the drawing of a great stone wheel that lies on the side of a mountain far north of here. From where your unimpeded wind comes, I suppose. A medicine wheel, Carrie calls it.

Gregory turns to him with interest.

GREGORY

Carrie? Carrie knows about such things?

WHERRITT

Well, all things Kiowa, you know. This is another of her fascinations. The grandfather of one of her pupils brought it to her. She sees fit to make it a subject of her classroom discussions. Sometimes her enthusiasm runs away with her, as I needn't tell you. With her it is sometimes difficult to tell who teaches and who is taught.

GREGORY

She, ah, takes herself too seriously at times? (*He turns to the wheel again and traces it with his fingers.*) Medicine wheel. It is a ring of stones, you say. And these are the spokes of the wheel.

WHERRITT

Stones.

GREGORY

And this hub?

WHERRITT

A stone well, as Carrie tells me.

GREGORY

There are knobs on the circumference, here and here and here.

WHERRITT

Cairns.

GREGORY

What does it mean, the medicine wheel?

WHERRITT

Ask Carrie. I've told you all I know. To me, frankly, it's superstition, paganism. Such things are sacrilegious, I believe.

GREGORY

Or sacred, as Carrie might say.

Wherritt returns to his writing, then in frustration crushes the sheet of paper in his hand and throws it on the floor. Stands. Gregory regards him.

GREGORY

What is that you are writing? If I may ask.

WHERRITT

It is nothing, a report.

GREGORY

(*immediately interested*) A report? Ah. A report. Ah, good. A report of, ah . . . I don't recall asking you to report. Is it . . .

WHERRITT

No, no. It has not been solicited . . . as yet. I was simply trying to set down in writing my responsibility as disciplinarian.

GREGORY

Well, but that responsibility is clearly spelled out in the manual, Barton. It is . . .

WHERRITT

Yes, yes, I know. Well, I simply wanted to know . . . wanted to express *my* reading, *my*, ah, interpretation of the manual. I . . . oh, it doesn't matter. It was an exercise; it is of no importance. (*Gregory is apparently disappointed. Before he can reply Wherritt changes the subject.*) You've come from the barn?

GREGORY

. . . all there in the manual. Uh, yes. The barn. I've just come from there.

WHERRITT

Has Emdotah come back?

GREGORY

No . . . no. It is so cold out there, Barton. I've never known it to be so cold. Four years ago there was a winter in Montana, they say. All the cattle died.

WHERRITT

Not back. God, it is strange.

GREGORY

The Great Plains of the North American Continent. Imagine.

WHERRITT

Too strange. He went after them this morning.

GREGORY

Yes. Before breakfast, even, wasn't it?

WHERRITT

Too strange. They couldn't have left much before daybreak. And he left just later, say an hour, or two at the most. On horseback. There must have been tracks.

GREGORY

Faint tracks, perhaps. Was it snowing then?

WHERRITT

Besides, he knew where they were bound. He knew exactly where they were going. He always knows.

GREGORY

Oh, he knew, for a fact. He always knows. He has eyes in the back of his head, he does. His boy Sailor, too. Like father, like

son. They have an extra sense, you know. Primitive, an instinct.
They always know. *(pause)*
    Listen, they had on warm clothing, hadn't they?

WHERRITT

(quickly) Oh, yes, warm clothing. Very warm clothing indeed.

GREGORY

Yes, I was sure they had. That would make a difference, wouldn't it? Warm clothing? Lord almighty, nothing to break the wind in a thousand miles.

WHERRITT

(as if reciting) Very warm indeed. Each wore an entire new suit of jeans clothes, a hickory shirt, a suit of heavy canton flannel underwear, a cap, a scarf, mittens, heavy socks, and boots. Yes, very warm, warm clothing, to my certain knowledge.

GREGORY

The Great Plains of the North American Continent. *(pause)*
    It would make a difference, wouldn't it—warm clothing?
(suddenly concerned) Damn it, Barton, what are we to do with the runaways? How can we prevent them?

He looks almost despairingly at Wherritt, who before answering walks across the stage, nearly upon the children. They look up at him with something like curiosity.

WHERRITT

We can't prevent them, Mr. Gregory. We can only punish them. It's not the same thing.

GREGORY

Punish them? *(He seems to weigh this briefly, sits at a teacher's desk.)*
You know, sometimes I think . . . You know, Barton, sometimes I think they are only children, after all, and . . .

WHERRITT

And children, when they misbehave, have to be punished. That is what we believe, isn't it, Mr. Gregory? It is our duty, according to the rules, according to the manual.

GREGORY

Yes, by God, it is! Truly. Our duty! *(He strikes the desk with his fist.)*
Our duty! Nothing less.

WHERRITT

As the Lord is our witness. We are sworn to do our duty. And I do mine, Mr. Gregory. So help me God, I do mine.

GREGORY

(*quickly*) Why, of course you do, Barton. Of course you do! We all know that. And there will be a commendation, I'm sure . . .

WHERRITT

I do mine, Mr. Gregory, and I did mine in this instance, I assure you. Sailor is a troublemaker. I punished him because he misbehaved. He deliberately violated the rules of the school, and it was my solemn *duty* to punish him. Discipline is my charge. I am "teacher and *disciplinarian*" of the Kiowa Boarding School. That is my title, sir, my official *title*.

GREGORY

(*inspired*) It is your very title, your . . . your *trust*, no less.

WHERRITT

Sailor is a troublemaker. He's a bully. He *likes* to abuse the little ones, to kick them about. He kicked the little sickly one, what's his name—Justin—in the stomach and made him cry. It must have hurt like hell. And so I laid the strap to him.

GREGORY

You were right to do so, Barton. You were right! Children, when they misbehave, have to be punished. Everyone understands that. It is written down. It is a matter of Boarding School policy, after all.

He rises and approaches close to Wherritt. Both appear to look at the children, but they do not see them. Clearly the children see them.

WHERRITT

Children, all of them.

GREGORY

What?

WHERRITT

They are all children. We are dealing with children, Mr. Gregory. Indians are children.

GREGORY

But you don't mean *all*, Barton. Look, Sailor is fifteen, as tall

WHERRITT

Because they are *children*.

GREGORY

(*confidentially*) You know, Barton, when I first came out here I had such . . . such *hopes*. Yes, and a kind of missionary zeal. I wanted to civilize the Indians. Well, I'm not a religious man, really, but I wanted to save their souls, too. (*pause*)

And then . . . and then I saw that it was wrong to hope so fervently. My hopes were dashed! There was bitter disappointment and frustration at every turn! I wanted to give up. You know, I saw in every schoolboy a leader, a good, hard-working, reputable man. Oh, I'm not talking about statesmen or heroes or saints. I'm talking about healthy, happy, productive human beings, people like you and me. Little George would become a farmer, Stephen a doctor, Henry a trader. But even as I looked at their dark, expressionless faces, they fell short. They couldn't live up to my most modest dreams. And I knew that I was thinking wrongly. It is not in them to be farmers; they have not, in all their generations on the earth, had an agricultural tradition. How can they be doctors, when sickness is their natural state and they fall like flies to every disease they are exposed to? They know nothing of money; they had rather deal in beads and bottles. To them a horse is the difference between rich and poor.

WHERRITT

I hadn't sensed your, ah, disappointment, your concern.

GREGORY

Wait, Barton, don't misunderstand me. Hear me out. I was naïve. I was not in touch with the reality of the situation, *their* reality.

WHERRITT

Reality? Their reality? Where in the name of God is *their* reality? Children do not care for reality, Mr. Gregory. They prefer make-believe. Why, right now they are probably dancing in the camps, the Ghost Dance. It's all make-believe. They are making believe that their dead will rise from their graves, that the buffalo will come back, that we whites will go away and leave them alone. Ha! *We* are their reality, Mr. Gregory, and they *will* come to know it.

---

and strong as I am. Oh, they are grown men at that age, Barton. You know, they mature more quickly than white people do, and they live shorter lives. And Sailor, with his white hair, is like an old man! What a spook he is with his scraggly white hair and his vacant eyes—there is no expression in them whatsoever. You never know what he is thinking. And that awful dent in his head! Do you know that when the Commissioner was here he looked at Sailor and didn't know what to say? I mean, what on earth *can* one say?—"Oh, dear, who is the freakish one, the one with the white hair and the hole in his head?" Do you know what one of the cooks told me?—she knows—she said that when Sailor was a little boy his hair just suddenly turned white, quite unaccountably. And the medicine man, trying to turn it back, hit Sailor over the head with a bottle of something, some oil or elixir, I suppose, just bang! And broke the bottle on his head and gave him that awful wound. Magic, I suppose, and of course it didn't work, didn't work at all. (*pause*)

But what were we talking about? Oh, yes, men, manhood. You said they were all children, and I had the sense that you meant *all*. There have been great chiefs, you know, men of wisdom and consequence. What about them? (*pause*)

But you were speaking in an ironic way, weren't you, Barton? I see. Well, if you mean maturity, intellectual maturity, sophistication, a sense of responsibility, moral responsibility, above all—well, God knows Sailor is no example. But what about some others? What about John Pai?

WHERRITT

Ah, yes, John Pai. I wondered when his name would come up. John Pai, the best student this school has ever had, John Pai, soon to be apostle to the Indians, the Kiowa messiah. They need one, God knows. We will address him as "Reverend," I suppose.

GREGORY

Well . . .

WHERRITT

He is an *Indian*. Indians are children. Children all—Sailor, John Pai, Rachel, Emdotah—children! Why, those indolent thieves and beggars, those dreamers out there in the camps, those poor, *befeathered*, war-painted Ghost Dancers are *children*! The old, pathetic ones with their rheumy eyes and running sores—those "wise men" are nothing but children. Don't you see? *(He catches himself, sees that he is out of control, pauses, continues in a different tone.)*

Don't you see, Mr. Gregory? They are children, the children of God. What *innocence*! Oh, what a state of innocence and grace! God bless them, they will surely inherit the earth. You know, Mr. Gregory, they are a worthy people. They deserve the best that we can give them, our very best, the highest expression of Christian charity that is in us. They are altogether worthy of our charity, the best that is in us.

GREGORY

Yes, oh yes. *(pause, then delicately)*

Do you . . . do you love them?

WHERRITT

(taken aback, then solemnly) Oh, I love them so.

GREGORY

And you want to save their souls, don't you?

WHERRITT

(ironically) Well, a bit out of my department, sir. I want John Pai, the right Reverend John Pai, to save their souls.

GREGORY

But . . .

WHERRITT

As for me, I want to make them fit in their heads and hands. I want to teach them to think, as far as they are able, to read and write, to know and respect the law of the land, to figure and keep accounts, to buy and sell. I want them to earn a decent living, earn it, I say. I want to teach them to paint and carpenter and husband and farm. I want them to be, by God, *Americans*, Mr. Gregory! I want them to feel at home in America! *(pause)*

We are entering upon the twentieth century, sir. It is our time, America's time. A time of greatness. Oh that is so clearly, excitingly true! Why can't they see it? Why do they resist that glorious destiny? Why do they *resist*?

GREGORY

Because they are different . . .

GREGORY

Well, but . . . as I was saying, I learned patience. I began to see the scheme of things. I began to trust in the judgment of my superiors. The United States Government, Barton, the Department of the Interior, the Office of Indian Affairs, the Indian School Service—these are the particular patches of a great and beautiful quilt, don't you know? And I began to see the proper order of this and that and the other, the arrangement and design, the symmetry and proportion. Yes, and I saw that if I held my attention squarely upon the business at hand, why, the whole scheme, all the meaner parts of the whole would fall into place. *(gloriously)* If we are to do this great work of bringing civilization to the frontier, Barton, we must do it a day at a time, and we must not lose heart. Our task will be done, our purpose served, our mission accomplished!

WHERRITT

In time?

GREGORY

In the fullness of time.

WHERRITT

I see. In time. In the fullness of time. What about the *nick* of time? Isn't the object of teaching these children to convert them, therefore to save them? And don't we mean to do it overnight, in the very nick of time? Wasn't that Mr. Pratt's idea of Fort Marion? Shackle the cream of the warrior crop, the poor beaten bastards, stuff them in a train, scare the shit out of them, then, in mercy, let them live in a prison that was called a hotel, give them ledger books and colored pencils, give them sticks and string to make bows and arrows, and allow them to sell their charming, primitive arts and crafts to benevolent, curious sightseers for money, honest-to-God coin of the realm. Give them the English language, Christian names, and gainful employment. Inform them politely that their gods have forsaken them and that their way of life is unacceptable, uncivilized, and poof!—the transformation. *(wearily)* Can we, Mr. Gregory, in the nick of time, do any better with the children?

GREGORY

(unsettled) But there is Carlisle, and . . .

WHERRITT

Worse! A *real* prison! My God, have you seen the photographs of the graves there? (*He takes out a watch from his pocket, reads the time.*) Your beautiful quilt, Mr. Gregory, your grand scheme, tell me, where are the boys in it, the runaways?

Gregory makes a brief gesture toward Wherritt, as if to give him aid.

GREGORY

You are worried about them, aren't you? I am, I can tell you. (*hesitantly*) You love them, don't you, Barton?

WHERRITT

I love them so.

There is a long moment in which their eyes meet and hold and break apart. They look to the door. At the same time there is an instant of the flute and voices echoing. The children stand and stiffen, peering, straining to hear.

WHERRITT

Did you hear something out there? Emdotah. Maybe he's back. I'm going to the barn.

GREGORY

I'm going with you.

They put on coats hurriedly and exit. The children sit, careless and composed. Blackout.

ACT ONE

Scene Two

The same room, moments later

The wheel, dimly illuminated. Soft spot up on children at desks stage right. "Foundation," Caldwell's Union Harmony (1837). Lights up, silhouetting the figure of John Pai. He moves slowly to the portrait of Lincoln, takes it in his hands, observes it intently.

JOHN PAI

Hello, Mr. Lincoln, Mr. President. Hello, or as we say in Kiowa, "*Get-aighah.*" Hello; how are you? I have been thinking. Do you know, Mr. Lincoln, I have been thinking of Miss Carrie. And do you know, Mr. Lincoln, I am beside myself. *(pause)*

I like the notion of being beside myself. We *Gaigwu*, we Kiowas, have a story, an old, holy story about hero twins. One boy threw up a gaming wheel. It came down and split him in two. He was two boys then, twins. He stood beside himself, you see. *(He turns the portrait from side to side, this way and that. He plays with it, makes it an indispensable part of his reverie.)* I have heard that there were times, Mr. Lincoln, when you were beside yourself. To tell you the truth, I care about that. It interests me, for I am truly beside myself. I am a red Indian. Perhaps you have heard of us red Indians, Mr. President. We are a savage race, rather good looking, tall, dark, stoic, fierce, uncivilized, often dangerous. In some books we are said to be noble. Mr. Pratt, who imprisoned some of my relatives in Florida, gave us a way to become civilized. I wonder if you, Mr. Lincoln, would approve. He has provided us with schools, schools in which we learn how to slough our red skins, forget our languages, forget our parents and grandparents, our little brothers and sisters, and our dead ancestors. School here, Mr. Lincoln, is a camp where the memory is killed. We must forget our past. Our existence begins with the cutting of our hair and the taking of a Christian name. Here at the Kiowa Boarding School at Anadarko, Oklahoma, on the banks of the Washita River, I am taught not to remember but to dismember myself. Well, Mr. Lincoln, I am beside myself, and I see my reflection in a pool of water or a pane of glass, and I wonder who I am. Was it so with you, Mr. Lincoln? Did you see your reflection and wonder who you were? They say that you knew about brothers killing brothers. We Kiowas can cry with you about that, Mr. Lincoln. The death of a brother is a hard thing. Seta and I, we are brothers. How can I tell you?—one of us must die. I am beside myself. I am a white man, am I not? It is perhaps not easy to tell. Look at me, Mr. Lincoln. When Miss Carrie looks at me, what does she see? What does she see in the Kiowa John Pai? I see in her a white woman. She is handsome, she is learned, she is well spoken, and she is kind. I think about her in ways a seminarian ought not, perhaps. This feeling: it is a state of grace, perhaps. Among uncivilized beings, I mean, among red Indians, among the indolent. You know, Mr. Lincoln, if I could just get back to the camps, with all my schooling, of course, and reacquaint myself with the old people and with the daughter of Tsentainte or with that tall girl from Saddle Mountain, I think I could be a fine, fine preacher. *Aiee!*

John Pai stands facing the wheel, concentrated, his back to the audience, his hands clasped behind him. Slowly he raises them outward and makes a circle of his arms around his head, describing the medicine wheel, just touching the tips of his middle fingers above him. In this position he makes an about face, drops his arms smartly to his sides with a slap, stands rigid at attention. He is standing inspection. His shoes are brightly shined, his collar clean and crisp, his trousers sharply creased, every hair in place. He wears a burgundy sweater with a large, white block letter "K" on the front.

    Music fades. Enter Carrie stage right. She appears older than her twenty-five years, but she is sensual and attractive, and she holds herself erect. Her hair is dark, fixed in a knot at the back of her head. She wears a long skirt, a white blouse with a cameo, and a shawl. She carries a sheaf of papers. She walks briskly in, does not at first notice John Pai (apparently), arranges the papers on the desk, begins to sit down. John Pai does a right face, toward her. She starts, catches her breath, remains standing. The children observe without particular interest.

CARRIE
    John!
JOHN PAI
    Sir! . . . Uh, Ma'am!
CARRIE
    You gave me a start. Have they come back, the boys?
JOHN PAI
    I don't know, ma' am.
CARRIE
    Emdotah?
JOHN PAI
    I don't know, ma'am. I saw Mr. Wherritt and Mr. Gregory

walking toward the barn a few minutes ago. Doing double
time, rather. I think they were cold.

CARRIE

I don't wonder. It's dreadful, the cold. (She studies him for a
moment, smiles.)

At ease, John. Relax. If they were back, you would know,
wouldn't you, John?

JOHN PAI

Yes, ma'am. We would all know, I think.

CARRIE

All? How? Why do you say that we would all know?

JOHN PAI

The KBS is a compact community, close-knit and efficient. Our
grapevine is both complex and compact.

CARRIE

Don't be impertinent.

JOHN PAI

No, ma'am. But it's true. The schoolchildren, they would
know.

The children nod and snigger in agreement.

CARRIE

And you can drop the "ma'am," which is inappropriate here
and now. (She sits at the desk, making a little seduction of her movements.) Under the circumstances, John, you can acknowledge
that we know each other as well as we do. (pause)

Yes, I believe what you say. The children know that three of
their number are missing, and they know who they are and,
very likely, where they are or where they are going, and they
would know, even the little ones, of their return. (She looks in the
direction of the children, who are now intent upon her words.) But not
one of them has said a word. Not one of them has said a word
or even mentioned the names of the missing ones, not one.

JOHN PAI

Without words or names, they would know.

CARRIE

You speak in riddles, John Pai. (brightly) Anyway, all that aside, I
have news. Good news. Very good news!

JOHN PAI

New York.

CARRIE

Yes! You've been accepted at seminary! (*He takes a step toward her.*)

Come here.

He approaches her and extends his hand somewhat awkwardly. She takes it, laughing, and pulls him closer.

JOHN PAI

This . . . this is an extraordinary day.

She releases him, still laughing.

CARRIE

Just think, John. You're the first from the Kiowa School, the very first and only! Why, you're going to put us on the map, do you realize that? Oh, wait till George—Mr. Gregory—hears, and Agent Adams, and your parents!

JOHN PAI

My parents . . .

CARRIE

They will be so proud! Oh, *congratulations*, John! What does it feel like, to have been chosen?

JOHN PAI

Thank you, ma'am—Miss Carrie. I am overwhelmed.

CARRIE

Goodness knows, I'm proud, I can tell you that. I think in these last few weeks I was as anxious to hear as you were.

JOHN PAI

You deserve the credit, ma'am. It was because of you. . . .

CARRIE

By no means! Your application was very strong, they say, *your* application. They speak of your originality, your command of the language, your eloquence.

JOHN PAI

Yours. I set your words down on the paper. I couldn't . . .

CARRIE

>Don't be impertinent. I was merely your, your intermediary.

JOHN PAI

>Imagine. I am eloquent, and it isn't even my native language.

CARRIE

>But you have taken possession of it, appropriated it, made it your own, as if you were born to it.

JOHN PAI

>I *was* born to words, truly, ma'am—very old words, from the time when dogs could talk.

CARRIE

>You will make a fine preacher, John. You will spread the gospel, as they say. You will glorify the word of God.

JOHN PAI

>The word of dog, the voice of the turtle.

CARRIE

>(*exasperated*) If we can get you past your impertinence! Your riddling is . . .

JOHN PAI

>Unseemly?

CARRIE

>Out of place. Remember yourself; you are almost no longer a schoolboy; you are almost a man of the cloth.

He steps back, glances at the wheel.

JOHN PAI

>I *do* remember myself: I was a camp child, a child of the cloth, trade cloth. I preached to the dogs in the name of the Sailor, the Dragonfly, and the Muchacho. Amen.

The children regard him closely.

CARRIE

>Oh, stop it, John! Just *stop* it! You're going to pop off with something like that in front of George or Agent Adams one of these times, and you're going to be in a sad lot of trouble.

JOHN PAI

>Will I be whipped?

CARRIE

> (*almost intimately*) I love to play at words with you. You know
> that. I love you to play with me . . . at words. But sometimes I
> think I've been wrong to encourage you.

JOHN PAI

> I love you to encourage me.

CARRIE

> It's just that I wanted for so long to find a student who, who
> could make use of me, total use, whose mind and sensitivity I
> could shape and sharpen, who would justify and fulfill me,
> who would confirm me in my purpose . . . in my person and . . .
> vocation. It is what every . . . teacher dreams of, John. And I
> found you.

*He regards again the wheel. Carrie slowly stands, closes her eyes and places her
hands in the hollow of her skirt, draws them up to her breasts. He is, and is not,
aware of her movements. The long moment is clandestine, sexual, beautiful.
And it is over.*

JOHN PAI

> You invented me. And I will be whipped?

They face each other.

CARRIE

> You don't realize how much you mean to me . . . to us. You're
> our entry, John, and our offering, our dearest sacrifice. You are
> what we've got to show for all the disappointment and frustra-
> tion of this place.

JOHN PAI

> This institution, this conversion factory, this experiment in
> camping. Ma'am, will I be whipped?

CARRIE

> (*explosively*) No! Now hear this! He wasn't whipped! Sailor
> wasn't *whipped!* Don't you see? He was merely *disciplined.*

JOHN PAI

> Excuse me, ma'am. Are we talking about hurt? Which is the
> most hurtful?

CARRIE

> Please, let's not play at words just now. You know what I mean. Sailor wasn't hurt.

JOHN PAI

> No?

CARRIE

> Physical pain was not inflicted upon him. Barton Wherritt couldn't whip anyone; he hasn't the stomach for it. It was . . . it was symbolic.

JOHN PAI

> Ah.

CARRIE

> And Sailor reacted out of petulance and spite, like a child. He overreacted. Look what he's done. He's taken two little boys out into the storm. He has put us all in harm's way.

JOHN PAI

> Harm's way. (pause)
>
> > Yes, I know that way.

CARRIE

> What?

JOHN PAI

> The way to the camps, the way they must have taken.

CARRIE

> West.

JOHN PAI

> Yes, west, across the river.

The children are animated, excited. Carrie moves toward them, distraught.

CARRIE

> Oh, dear God, the river! I didn't think of the river! Could they have crossed it?

JOHN PAI

> Yes. It is low in winter. But it is harm's way.

CARRIE

> They could have walked across?

JOHN PAI

> There's not a bridge close by, but they could have waded

across. It would be nothing for a man on a horse. Emdotah
must have crossed it easily. Arch, Koi-khan-hodle, would have
flown across on a horse.

CARRIE

But they hadn't horses. They had to get their feet wet.

JOHN PAI

Yes, they probably had to break through ice near the banks.

CARRIE

But they could have dried their feet, couldn't they. They could
have thought to take their boots and socks off, to keep them
dry. And they could have taken towels—has anyone counted
towels? And they could have got help, maybe. They could have
taken the Wichita–Fort Sill road. There might have been trav-
elers. There might even have been friends, family.

JOHN PAI

No. They were running away, and they were afraid. They kept
well away from the road.

She turns to him sharply.

CARRIE

But how can you know that?

JOHN PAI

Do you suppose I never ran away?

*She is struck dumb for a moment, incredulous. She looks at him closely,
suspiciously.*

CARRIE

You, John Pai. No, I don't believe it for a minute.

JOHN PAI

And do you know, ma' am, it was worth it. When I reached my
mother's camp it was as if I had returned from the dead. I was so
glad to be there, and everyone was so glad to see me. We wept
with gladness. The old people, my grandparents, my mother
and father, even the children wept. We wanted to touch, and we
touched each other. We touched so softly, so gladly, the way very
old, blind people touch the babies. And then we talked, all at

once, and it wasn't talk somehow, but it was sounds and si-
lences and singing and weeping, some old, jumbled expression
of our being: Eh neh neh neh. And it seemed to me that the whole
world was there in the time being. And it didn't matter that I
would be hunted down and taken back, because the time being
was everything I ever wanted. It was all that my heart could hold.
The old free life of the Gaigwu was there, just there, and it was
mine, as it had been when I was born. I was simply, wholly,
joyfully alive for the first time in years. My spirit had been
caught and caged, and I had set it free again. Do you know how?
By running away, like those three boys, by returning, by going
home. Just the sheer physical exertion of running, of moving
like a wild animal over the earth, across rivers and creeks,
through woods, on the long, rolling plain—that was to be alive,
that was to be who I am and where I ought to be. And the camp!
The living, shining, jubilant camp! That night I ate the food for
which I had hungered so long, and I sang and danced, and there
was a give-away in my honor. I slept on the ground in a tepee,
and it was luminous under the moon, and there were coyotes
away on the high ground and crickets and frogs close by, and I
could hear even in my sleep the breathing of those I loved most
in the world. And I awoke before daylight and went out, still full
of the wonder of homecoming, and from a high stand of brush
and willows I watched the camp take shape in the first light.
And then an old man, old man Tanedah, came out of his tepee
and walked toward me. He came to a little rise in the ground,
and he stood there and lifted his arms, and he began to pray
aloud. And in that moment, when he lifted his voice to the sky,
the morning broke, and the world began to burn in a low golden
light. Then his skin was glowing in the golden light, and I saw
that his face was thin and wrinkled, and it was painted blue and
yellow and white, and his eyes were very black and bright, and
his voice carried on the long wind, became one with the cold,
purling wind of the morning. It carried all the way to the rising
sun, I believe. I do believe it. (pause)

That old man's clear voice on the clear morning. It was un-
speakably old and holy, older and holier than Genesis. (pause)

And the policeman from the school came and took me back.

There is a long moment in which the children lay their heads on their desks.
Carrie clears her throat.

CARRIE

(*lowly*) And then?

JOHN PAI

I was disciplined.

CARRIE

You were . . . whipped?

JOHN PAI

That was the least of it. Physical pain was not inflicted upon
me. It was symbolic, it was merely the pain of humiliation.
Shame. I was made to do what I had to do when I first came to
the school, as a little boy. They cut my hair, which was already
cut short. They left cuts and little tufts of hair on my scalp. That
is how we *Gaigwu* look when we are grieving. It was as if I was
mourning my own death. Then I had to stand naked with the
new students, who were much younger than I and terribly
frightened, who thought that they were being put to death,
while we were deloused with poisonous powder; it got into our
eyes and nostrils and mouth. And then I had to choose again
my Christian name from a list on the blackboard, pointing
with a stick. It was like counting coup. My name was my enemy. How is it you say?—I was made an example.

Carrie studies John Pai as if she is memorizing him. He is lost in thought.
She comes to him, places a hand upon his arm.

CARRIE

John?

JOHN PAI

Ma' am.

CARRIE

John, do you remember last spring, the picnic below the Agency?

JOHN PAI

Yes, I do.

CARRIE

The redbud trees were in blossom. The air was sweet, wasn't it?
It was the first really pretty day of the year, wasn't it?

JOHN PAI

> There were people from the camps. They tied bright ribbons to the trees and fence posts. There were bright blankets on the grass. It was like a Sun Dance. You wore a yellow dress . . . ma' am.

CARRIE

> Did I? Yes, I did. My mother sent it to me. (pause)
>
> John, the willow ring. I have it.

JOHN PAI

> The willow ring, yes.

CARRIE

> The beautiful hoop you made with the leather strings, like a cat's cradle.

JOHN PAI

> The gaming wheel. Sailor made it.

CARRIE

> Yes, Sailor. And the two of you were playing with it, rolling it on the grass and thrusting sticks at it—I think you were showing off, but you were very skillful, I remember. I remember it so clearly. The wheel rolling, and you running after it, beside it, and it rolled so prettily on the grass, among the wildflowers, and the leather lace spinning, and the little ring in the center, where the strings were all strung together, it was small, wasn't it? (She makes a ring with her thumb and forefinger.) And you thrust your stick right into the little ring. (She moves her other forefinger into the ring.) It was remarkable, really. Really remarkable.

JOHN PAI

> It was like the Sun Dance. There were singers from the camps. The sun shone and the gaming wheel rolled. And we ran with arrows, Sailor and I. (pause)
>
> Physical pain was not inflicted upon me. It was symbolic. It was merely the pain of humiliation.

Blackout.

ACT ONE

Scene Three

The same room, a short time later

The wheel, dimly lighted. Spots dimly on Lincoln portrait and on Carrie seated at desk. John Pai is barely silhouetted stage left, standing perfectly still, looking into space. Carrie is writing. After a long moment the light brightens on her. She puts down the pen and picks up the page, and she reads aloud.

CARRIE

Dear Mama, I miss you, miss you. It is so good to have your letters. You know, you are the only one who writes to me on a regular basis. I so crave to have news of home and of my family, of those I love most in the world. I am well, and my life here is full. It seems especially full just now. We are all on edge. Three of our schoolboys ran away, and as of this moment they have not been found. You cannot imagine how this demoralizes us. You cannot imagine how quiet and somber the children have become. We, all of us here, keep brave faces, but our hearts tremble. The worst of it is that the weather is as hard as I've seen in the territory. We had a blizzard yesterday; the snow drove into the night, and there came a cold like death. Even inside I shiver to think of it! One of the boys is only eight years old. He is dear and funny and makes me laugh. Oh, how we fear for their safety! We are sitting on pins and needles. But there is good news, too. John Pai, of whom I have written you before, has been accepted at seminary. He is perfectly deserving, and we are so proud of him. Mr. Gregory fairly struts with pride—you should see him; he looks as if he's just had a mouthful of your Christmas cobbler! John Pai is going to be a wonderful preacher, mother, and he is going to put the Kiowas on the Jesus way! I guess I am sounding now like a missionary, which I know must please you. Well, I still deliberate and pray as hard as I can for guidance. When I came here, mama, I was moved by an uncommon zeal. I wanted—and want—so much, more than I

can say, to save the Indians. But from time to time my zeal
declines, and I become confused. I begin to think of saving
myself, of saving my own soul. In the night, sometimes, I
question whether or not I am entitled to assist—or intervene—
in the salvation of their souls, their Indian souls. Sometimes it
occurs to me as a possibility that they have a greater possession
of their souls than I have of mine. I know that my commitment
to the Kiowa children is real and great. I love my work, but it is
hard and routine and thankless. (*This is as much as she has written.
She sets the page down and goes on.*)

And then, mama, there is a part of me that is, how shall I
say, sometimes *excited*. Do you know what I mean? I'm sure you
do, though we've never talked about it. I am a grown woman,
and I am hale and alone and restless. Mr. Gregory looks at me
sometimes. Barton Wherritt and John Pai look at me sometimes. I am aware of it, mother. I am aware of it. You know, the
yellow dress you sent to me is a thing I cherish above all my
other belongings, except my Bible. I wrote to you about the
picnic. I think I may wear it soon again, when we send John Pai
off to the seminary. I don't have in all my memories a better day
than I lived at the picnic, in the yellow dress. I could be married
in it, mama. I shall keep it, and take it wherever I go, so that I
can be married in it, when the time comes, to the man, who-
ever he is, who shall be my husband forever and forever. Your
loving daughter, Carrie.

*Lights up on classroom. Spot up on seated children. A horse neighing in the
distance. There is commotion outside. Carrie rises. John Pai springs forward.
Enter from outside Gregory, Wherritt, and Emdotah. They do not remove their
coats. The children jump to their feet and are extremely alert. All eyes are on
Emdotah. He is dumb and expressionless. He is in dirty work clothes—overalls,
boots, a stiff, tattered duster, a shapeless hat. He stands downstage right near
the children. He removes his hat, crumples and holds it tightly in his hands. His
long braids are wrapped in ticking. His attitude, physical and emotional, is
that of a prisoner.*

CARRIE
    What?

WHERRITT

So.

GREGORY

There will have to be a report. Immediately.

CARRIE

Emdotah!

Emdotah's eyes remain downcast; he gives no sign of hearing. The children peer up at him, squinting their eyes.

GREGORY

There will have to be a report, of course. Immediately. A complete report. This is the most extraordinary behavior.

CARRIE

(to Emdotah) You brought them back? How are they? Where?

Emdotah stands mute.

WHERRITT

Yes, indeed, where are they?

John Pai, like the children, has taken a remarkable interest in Emdotah from the moment he came in. John Pai watches him intently, slowly moves close to him, peers into him.

WHERRITT

Our trusted scout Emdotah apparently doesn't know where they are any more than we do. My God, Carrie, he's been here all day! He went out this morning, hot on their trail, crossed the river, and came back! He gave up at the river! Then he came back and has been the whole day with the animals, keeping warm in some cozy corner of the barn with the goddamned animals! Not a word to anyone! Just tra la la la la, the everyday chores. When Mr. Gregory and I went to the barn we found him sitting there in the straw, singing, for God's sake! Sitting there, in the dark, singing! Singing!

CARRIE

Oh!

JOHN PAI

(to Emdotah, softly) I know the song.

GREGORY

Extraordinary! Certainly a complete report.

WHERRITT

Where are they, indeed.

JOHN PAI

(just audibly) They are camping.

The children sit and slump.
Blackout.

ACT ONE

Scene Four

Flute and voices echoing. Dim light up on children, who are like small animals before an earthquake. Spot on John Pai, Emdotah, and Mother Goodeye. The stage is vague, misty, a dream dimension. John Pai is asleep in chair. At his feet are three sleeping forms in blankets. They are like mummies or body bags, bundles of soft definition.

MOTHER GOODEYE

Eh neh neh neh! Look, Emdotah, he dreams them.

EMDOTAH

And they dream us, grandmother. We are a dream in the heads of children.

MOTHER GOODEYE

I cannot see them, whether or not their faces are sweet and peaceful—the white-haired, original boy, the one who is good with horses, who will have a famous shield, and the little, big-bellied one. But they are here, aren't they?

EMDOTAH

If they are not here, grandmother, then neither are we.

MOTHER GOODEYE

Here is Seta, your favorite son, Emdotah.

EMDOTAH

Here, sleeping. I cannot see his face, whether or not it is sweet and peaceful, his white, wounded head. Oh my son!

MOTHER GOODEYE

Here is the son of Territory Horse and the son of Muchacho. Here, sleeping. Oh my grandsons!

Emdotah moves close over the bundles, looks down at them.

EMDOTAH

Children: I want to speak to you. I want to place my words upon you now, now that you have gone away, into the darkness. That darkness is a world I do not know, though I shall know it. I have heard the old people are there. I have heard that my mother and father are there, and my grandmothers and my grandfathers, and theirs, and theirs. It must be a wonderful place, like the green floor of Palo Duro Canyon, if all those old, beloved ones are there, if they are there. When I come, I want to see them close. I want them to stand around me. I want them to greet me and tell me that they are glad to see me. I shall be who I am then. I shall not be then an agency Indian; I shall not wear these ugly, branded clothes. And I shall not hunt down my children! I shall have lived as I could, and I shall be with you in the right way, in the right spirit. And you, my children, is it so with you? Is the darkness safe? Are the old ones there to take you in, to make you feel at home? Certainly they are. In my mind's eye, and in my heart, I see you moving into the camps, not the poor camps, not the camps of the time when the ponies are killed, not the time of the camps when the buffalo are gone. But the camps of the *Gaigwu*, the coming-out people, in their gladness, in their dignity, in their glory.

I want to place my words upon you now, now that you have gone away, into the darkness.

He raises his face, eyes closed. He lifts his arms and prays. Mother Goodeye and John Pai and the children repeat the word Aho ("thanks" in Kiowa) throughout.

Darkness,

You are, forever.

Aho.

You are, before the light.

Aho.

You stain the long ledge above the seep at Leaning

Walls.

Aho.

You are the smoke of silence burning.

Aho.

Above, below, beyond, among the glittering things, you

are.

Aho.

The days descend in you,

yesterday,

today,

the day to die.

Aho.

Aho.

Aho.

Aho.

MOTHER GOODEYE

Here is the son of Territory Horse. Here is the son of Mucha-cho. Here is the son of Emdotah. Oh, my grandsons! Here is the schoolboy John Pai, dreaming. Here is the Reverend John Pai, dreaming. *Eh neh neh neh!*

Blackout.

END OF ACT ONE

ACT TWO

Scene One

Some days later, evening

Snow falling on black stage left. Wheel dimly lighted. Children still and barely visible. Momentary flute and voices echoing. Spot on Mother Goodeye. Her right hand supports her weight on the stick. The other hand, which she holds up to her breast, is partially covered with a bloody rag, for she has cut off two fingers to express her grief. She speaks slowly, lowly at first.

MOTHER GOODEYE

It is a long way to the outer camps, a whole day for a man on a good horse in good weather, you see. For three children on foot in winter . . . this winter . . . *(long pause)*

They came to the near camps, but there are only the hang-around-the-Agency Indians, who would send them back— "Oh, you bad boys! You are schoolboys now. Go back to school and speak English!" Those goddam hang-around-the-Agency Indians. They pour Lilac Vegetal on their heads, and they smell like bad meat. But that is another story. I tell it to you some-time. *(pause)*

Oh, little Mosatse! Oh, little Kon', little grandson! He must have been so tired! But he did not want to go back to the school. He did not want to be whipped, you see. *(The children attend.)*

And Koi-khan-hodle, Dragonfly. His people live in one of the farthest camps—they can hear wolves in the mountains— and one of his grandmothers died just a little while ago, and Koi-khan-hodle wanted to go there and grieve for her in the proper way. Had he been alone he might have taken a horse, any horse, and made his way surely and swiftly. You know, he could make an old tired horse run like hell. Oh, on the back of a black-eared hunting horse he might have dreamed his shield!

He did not want to go back. He did not want to be whipped, you see. *(pause)*

And Seta, the old and crazy boy, the wild, white-headed boy. Those years at the school and nothing to show for it but a terrible loneliness and anger. He did not want to be whipped, you see. He did not want to be whipped again. No. Well, not the day they ran away, but the next, or the next, they lost their way, and a great storm came upon them. They were found frozen on a steep slope in the red hills far south of the Washita. Their own people, the people from the farthest camps, found them. There is a spring at that place, in a wall of rock, overgrown with brush. It is a holy place, you see. In the summer you can see it from far away, rising out of the yellow plain. Well, another boy, a living boy from the outer camps, rode to the Agency and to the Kiowa Boarding School and reported that schoolboys had been found, frozen to death. *(She regards her injured hand and says very softly:)* Frozen to death. Oh, my grandsons!

Blackout. Spots on Gregory and Wherritt, stage left and stage right, facing each other. Gregory holds two letters, reads from the first. This sequence of readings from documents can be very dry. It must be enlivened by the reactions of each man to the other (gestures of approval and encouragement, for the most part; perhaps some questioning or skepticism). The children, too, might be of help here. The idea is that the two men are bringing their respective reports of the incident into agreement. They want to present in their separate reports a unified and unassailable account.

GREGORY

Charles E. Adams, U.S. Indian Service, Kiowa Agency, Oklahoma. Sir: I have received with great regret yours of the 20th ultimo reporting the freezing to death of three runaway pupils from the Kiowa school. I desire a more circumstantial report of the facts. Please ask Mr. Gregory to furnish an explicit statement giving the names of the boys, the offense committed, the circumstances, and the exact nature and extent of the punishment. I would also like a statement in his own handwriting from the teacher and disciplinarian giving his version of the

matter. This is a most lamentable affair. . . . Very respectfully,
T. J. Morgan, Commissioner.

(*He clears his throat officiously, shifts letters, reads from the second:*)
The Honorable, The Commissioner of Indian Affairs, Washington, D.C. Sir: . . . One of the children at the Kiowa School was chastised in a mild manner. . . . Nothing much was thought of the circumstances at the time. A few days later, after the children had received new socks, boots, clothing, etc., this boy induced two others to run away with him. . . . A heavy snow, fully eight inches, fell, and they were found frozen to death, about forty miles from the Agency. . . . This affair is to be regretted from another standpoint: [the Kiowas] will always bring the matter up when asked for children for the schools, but I trust that it will grow out of their minds, if not their hearts. Very respectfully, Your obedient servant, Charles E. Adams, Indian Agent.

(*He lowers letters, sets himself in thought, begins to compose his report.*) Sir: . . . When they left the school each wore a full new suit of jeans clothing, given them only the day before—hickory shirt—suit of canton flannel underwear, heavy socks, boots, cap, scarf, and mittens . . .

Wherritt, too, begins to compose his report.

WHERRITT

Sir . . . The cause that prompted their departure from the school has never been definitely ascertained but is supposed to have been *partially* due to punishment inflicted by myself upon Sailor, on the morning of January 7th. . . .

GREGORY

. . . The time they perished is only conjecture, as the first body was not found until the following Wednesday. . . . Jack, the youngest, gave up first. When found he had his coat off and tied around his waist by the sleeves. Arch was found some little distance on. He had on neither coat nor shirt. Sailor's body was found about half a mile further away under an overhanging rock on the side of the mountain. He had taken off Arch's coat and shirt, ripped them, and had them on under his own. . . . All were buried without Christian rites. . . .

WHERRITT

At the time the boys left the school (to my certain knowledge) their apparel consisted of the following: each, an entire new suit of jeans clothes, (given them by myself the day previous to their departure), hickory shirt, suit of heavy canton flannel underwear; cap, scarf, mittens, heavy socks and boots.

GREGORY

Sailor had been in school about six years. Arch, a year and a half, and Jack three years. I remember your noticing Sailor while you were here. He had gray hair and a scar on his forehead. His father told me the medicine man tried to change the color of his hair by breaking a bottle containing a liquid, over his head. Since then he has been very cowardly, especially after nightfall. When badly frightened he seemed to be perfectly wild, and it would be some time before he would regain his presence of mind. I believe if it had not been for Sailor's great fright at the strange shapes that trees, shrubs, et cetera, took on at night when covered with snow, they would not have lost their way—and in a section inhabited by their own tribe, the location of whose camps they knew so well, they would have reached some camp before perishing.

WHERRITT

Judging from the *frequency* with which the *boys in question* ran away, I consider the principal incentive that led to their departure was identical with former instances; that is, they wanted to go to camp, preferring to reside there in indolence, rather than at school, leading a life of activity and usefulness.

GREGORY

Very respectfully, G.P. Gregory, Superintendent

WHERRITT

Very respectfully yours, Bart Wherritt, Teacher and Disciplinarian

Blackout.

ACT TWO

Scene Two

The next morning

Harmonica, "Got to Travel On." The children are playful, animated. Lights up on classroom. Carrie and Wherritt. She is prettily dressed and made up, as if to meet a beau. He is haggard and gaunt, in the same drab attire. There is a high tension in him, apparent in the stiffness of his stance and movements. He stands sideways to her, peers out the window. She carries an odd-shaped package, places it carefully on the desk, meanders slowly about the room as if he were not there.

CARRIE

> *(singing)* Black smoke's arisin',
> Yonder comes a train,
> Yonder comes a train,
> Yes, yonder comes a train.
> Black smoke's arisin',
> Yonder comes a train,
> And I feel like I gotta travel on.
> *(She stops, regards Wherritt saucily.)* Know what, Barton?

Wherritt turns to Carrie abruptly, with visible irritation.

WHERRITT
> What?

CARRIE
> Guess what.

WHERRITT
> Oh, for God's sake; what is it?

CARRIE
> I have something on my mind.

He looks at her warily, but with real interest. There is a moment in which he considers all possibilities. There is a lascivious shadow on his face.

WHERRITT

You have?

CARRIE

Yes.

WHERRITT

Ah, what is it?

CARRIE

Picnics.

WHERRITT

Picnics?

CARRIE

Picnics. Warm green grass, redbud trees, lemonade.

WHERRITT

(*exasperated*) Lemonade? Jesus, Carrie, it's the middle of winter!

CARRIE

(*singing*) Summer's almost gone,

Yes, winter's coming on.

She drops her head abruptly, clasps her hands and shudders, as if she is about to cry. He regards her for a moment with mixed emotions—anger, frustration, hurt, desire.

WHERRITT

It's John, isn't it? John Pai. He's leaving. You're sorry to see him go.

CARRIE

No!—well, sad and glad. It's a good thing for him—his gain, our loss.

WHERRITT

Your loss especially, I suppose. I know how you feel about him. *Your* loss.

CARRIE

Oh, Lord, Barton, we're racking up losses here, aren't we? Just now. It's a season for loss.

WHERRITT

(*sharply*) Nonsense! (*pause, awkwardly*) I mean . . . you mean, the dead boys, those things happen. It was an accident, that's all. You could see it coming.

She studies him.

CARRIE

    I couldn't.

WHERRITT

    (with rhetoric) Well, look here, Carrie. If you think about it, it was
    bound to happen.

CARRIE

    What are you saying?

WHERRITT

    Why, you know as well as I do that Sailor was to blame. If it
    weren't for his fear and craziness, his . . . well, those poor boys
    would have been alive today.

CARRIE

    His fear and craziness, his . . .

WHERRITT

    Let's be honest, he is an Indian, a savage.

CARRIE

    What *are* you saying? Fear and craziness, savagery? It sounds as
    if you're making an accusation, Barton, accusing that poor boy
    of a heinous crime. Next you'll be talking murder, or . . . or
    suicide, infanticide!

WHERRITT

    I will say it plainly—cowardice.

CARRIE

    Ah, so. Cowardice. You, Barton Wherritt, are talking about
    cowardice. I see.

WHERRITT

    Others are saying it.

CARRIE

    Cowardice and craziness and blame and savagery. It is a heavy
    charge, Barton. You lay it with authority. *(He signals her to lower
    her voice.)* I wonder, why can't you just let the dead be?

WHERRITT

    (a little wildly) There has to be blame . . . hasn't there? Of course,
    there has to be blame. *(with tired rhetoric)* Just consider what he
    did, Carrie. He convinced Arch and Jack to go with him. He
    might even have threatened them with harm if they didn't mind

him. Oh, he was good at that. He liked to kick the little ones, you know. And he led them to the first camps, but he wouldn't let them stay there, oh, no. He made them go on into the wild, dangerous country. And in the night they were all afraid and desperate, and the storm fell. And he took—stole—the clothes from the little ones, and who knows if they were dead or alive, or if they resisted him, and he left them behind and sought shelter to save himself. Himself, Carrie. And it did him no good. You can see that he was to blame, Carrie. Surely you can see that.

CARRIE

The Kiowas too?

For a moment there is a look of terror in his face.

WHERRITT

The Kiowas? Why, yes, of course. They can see it, too. They know.

CARRIE

It seems they always know.

WHERRITT

(*almost inaudibly*) They always know. (*pause*)
 But we must take great care, nonetheless.

CARRIE

Great care? What have we to fear?

WHERRITT

To fear. Why, nothing to fear. Of course we have nothing . . .

CARRIE

Reprisal?

WHERRITT

(*too quickly*) Reprisal? Whose? Against whom? Don't be ridiculous.

CARRIE

What is cooking in the camps, I wonder.

Wherritt steps close to window, looks out intently, searching for a long moment, turns to her.

WHERRITT

Your . . . John would know, wouldn't he? John Pai?

CARRIE

I'm sure he would, John and the others. They know. They always know.

WHERRITT

Just out of curiosity, Carrie, does he ever speak to you of me?

CARRIE

Of you? (*pause*)

   Why, no, I don't think so. He hasn't much to say about people. And he certainly doesn't talk about them behind their backs.

WHERRITT

No, no. Heavens no. I meant nothing of the sort. I merely wonder at times if he thinks well of me, that's all. He's such an upstanding young man, altogether admirable indeed. I would like him to think well of me, as I do of him, as he clearly thinks well of you.

CARRIE

We are often of a mind, John Pai and I. We see eye to eye on most issues.

WHERRITT

No doubt. Yes, no doubt he speaks well of you to the other students, and to the parents. Does he speak well of me, do you think?

CARRIE

Oh, he speaks well—like an orator. And I believe he speaks his mind.

WHERRITT

Yes. Well, he must be excited to be going off to seminary. What an adventure for an Indian. Imagine!

CARRIE

Imagine.

WHERRITT

(*resigned*) Do you know, Carrie, I've been thinking of going off myself, oh, just for a few days. I've got sick leave coming, and to tell the truth I've been under the weather lately, a bit off my feed, as they say. You know, I think it's the blasted wind. It comes down from the north, a thousand miles. Imagine. The Great Plains of the North American Continent.

CARRIE

> It would do you good to get away, Barton. You don't look well at all.

>> (aside, singing) Done laid around and stayed around
>> This ol' town too long,
>> And I feel like I gotta travel on.

WHERRITT

> Carrie.

CARRIE

> Yes, Barton?

WHERRITT

> Carrie, I would like to speak frankly.

Her interest is piqued.

CARRIE

> Would you?

WHERRITT

> Yes. You see, Carrie, I am somewhat on edge, under a certain amount of stress. The events of these last few days, well, they have taken their toll.

CARRIE

> And you are of a delicate constitution.

WHERRITT

> Well, no. Well, yes. But that is beside the point. The point is, I am thinking of leaving the Indian School Service by and by, well, at the end of this term, perhaps. I feel that I have another work to do. As you know, I am a man who wants to give of himself completely. I do not feel entirely useful here. Well, Carrie, I am moved to ask you if you are happy here.

CARRIE

> Ummm, more or less. Why do you ask, Barton?

WHERRITT

> Well, in a way this is about you and this place, Carrie.

CARRIE

> Me? And this place?

WHERRITT

> It's an unnatural place for a woman.

CARRIE

Yet women seem to thrive here.

WHERRITT

I'm talking about women, womenfolk, Carrie, not about squaws.

CARRIE

What is behind all this, Barton? What do you want with me?

WHERRITT

I want you to come away with me.

CARRIE

Thank you. No.

WHERRITT

Why not? (*He goes over the edge.*) It's John Pai, isn't it? (*He tries desperately to control his speech.*) John Pai is an Indian! John Pai is a schoolboy! You, Carrie, you're a woman, a white woman! You're a teacher, you're older, you're of . . .

CARRIE

Not yet of another generation, I hope. I am twenty-five, and I am an old maid. I have this mind, this body, these dreams, and this place, and I am an old maid. Let me tell you this, Bart, if I were in Philadelphia it would be otherwise.

WHERRITT

(*strangely desperate*) Come with me.

CARRIE

Thanks. No.

He is agonized, humiliated; he struggles to regain his composure.

WHERRITT

John Pai. Does he speak well of me?

Enter Gregory. He is jovial, almost smug, jaunty. Carrie and Wherritt look disinterested, but they cannot quite hide the fact that they have been engaged in private conversation.

GREGORY

Ah, a faculty tête-à-tête, is it? Are you a committee?

WHERRITT

> Hello. Ah, we . . . we were just discussing the remarkable good fortune of our Master John Pai, so well deserved.

GREGORY

> Hear! Hear! For he is a jolly good fellow!

CARRIE

> Hail to the seminarian. He does us proud. *(pause)*
>
> Oh, I don't know how to feel about his leaving us!

GREGORY

> Ah, on that very subject: I've just been to see Agent Adams. He asks that you, Carrie, come with John Pai to the Agency as soon as possible to make travel arrangements. There are forms, you know, requisitions, allowances, per diem, Government Issue, et cetera, et cetera, et cetera, in duplicates and triplicates. God, it's wonderful, isn't it? Arrangements, forms, orders, procedures, *proper* procedures. In a word, *efficiency!* We inhabit an age of order and efficiency!

CARRIE

> Oh, as soon as possible. John is to meet me here at any minute. I've a going-away present for him.

WHERRITT

> No doubt. *(to Gregory)* You have spoken with Agent Adams, Mr. Gregory? Just now, you say?

GREGORY

> Yes, indeed. I've just come from his office. It was a very cordial exchange. A gracious man, a gentleman, Agent Adams.

WHERRITT

> Excuse me, Mr. Gregory. Did he speak of the, ah, situation? What is Agent Adams' view of the present *situation*, I wonder.

GREGORY

> Situation.

CARRIE

> *(ironically)* The matter of the deceased boys, the frozen boys and their friends and relatives, he means. The Kiowas. *That* situation.

Wherritt tosses her a hateful glance.

GREGORY

Oh, that, yes. *(pauses, gathers himself)*

His view is that we have done our duty, Barton. We have acquitted ourselves with dignity and dispatch. I indicated to him in no uncertain terms the character of my report to the Commissioner, and of course I assured him that your own would be in the same spirit. He was genuinely pleased. Indeed, how could he not have been? The matter of the poor, unfortunate runaways has been set straight. We have been thorough, we have been candid and direct, we have been entirely professional, in a word.

CARRIE

(aside) We have been unimaginative and insensitive, in two words.

WHERRITT

It is finished then?

GREGORY

Quite. Quite finished.

CARRIE

George, isn't there some possibility of reprisal? Barton and I were in mind of that. The schoolchildren say there is anger in the camps.

(The children verify this in their attention and in their gestures.)

They know of it; they always know.

GREGORY

Nonsense. Reprisal? Whose? Against whom? Believe me, my dear, that sad affair is finished. We have put it to rest once and for all. And there is a moral in it, believe me. What is it that our friend and example, Mr. Pratt, says of his famous Carlisle School? He has a slogan, and a very clever and inspirational one it is, too. I can't quite bring it to mind.

CARRIE

Yes, he says, "Kill the Indian and save the man."

GREGORY

(flustered) Well, ah, no, no. I had another slogan in mind, clearly in mind. There was another saying, yes, there was definitely another saying, very clever. It was, ah, very clever and just to the point, as I recall.

WHERRITT

(aside) They know. They always know.

Enter John Pai. He nods to the others and belies nothing. His expression, as usual, is benign and inscrutable. The others greet him heartily, especially Wherritt. John Pai stands near Carrie, after taking a kind of customary observation of the wheel. The children pay him their attention.

GREGORY

So, what have you to say for yourself, John, on this auspicious occasion?

JOHN PAI

I, I am thankful.

GREGORY

Yes, yes, yes. But this is your particular triumph. You mustn't be humble. You are entitled to celebrate!

JOHN PAI

I was glad. And then came the terrible news that my brothers died in the snow, and now I have no heart for celebration. I am in mourning.

GREGORY

Then you will be glad to know that we have put the sad, distasteful events of that close time behind us. And so must you. Give it all good riddance, my boy. You have a bright future to look after.

JOHN PAI

Yes, sir.

CARRIE

John, your travel papers are being processed at the Agency. We must go there, as soon as we are finished here.

JOHN PAI

Finished. Yes, ma'am.

Wherritt steps quickly to John Pai.

WHERRITT

John, John, we are so very happy for you. You know, I envy you the long train ride through the countryside. It will be a wonder-

ful experience for you. There is so much to see, to take in. You
will have a real look at America. Have you ever been on a train?

JOHN PAI

No, I haven't, as you might know. One of my uncles rode on a
train. But he was a prisoner in chains, and he was sick and
afraid.

WHERRITT

Listen, John. I feel so bad about the boys who ran away. I want
you to know that, and I want you to express my deepest sympa-
thy to their families. Will you do that, can you?

CARRIE

Barton, he will not see them before he leaves.

JOHN PAI

(to himself) Arch, Koi-khan-hodle, wanted to go to the camps to
mourn, to grieve in the proper way.

WHERRITT

But you can get word to them, I'm sure. It is important to me
that they know how I feel. The boys were very dear to me.

JOHN PAI

And they, Mr. Wherrit, were always mindful of you.

WHERRITT

Yes. We seem to have established a rapport, a real bond.

JOHN PAI

They knew of bonds.

WHERRITT

Sailor, especially, was a young man I came to be fond of, in spite
of his misconduct. Mind you, I never considered his transgres-
sions willful. I understood perfectly, well, his, ah, disability.

JOHN PAI

Seta was not like the others, not even in the camps was he like
the others. He was old, one of the old people.

WHERRITT

Exactly. It is a disease. I have read of it, and of course you have
not had access to the books on the subject. There are cases in
which children have become senile, and they have died of old
age. Their hair turns white, and they babble and wither.

JOHN PAI

It seems Seta died of the cold, and perhaps of shame.

WHERRITT

> It is clear that Sailor acted imprudently, irrationally. He, well, he acted cowardly, it is sad to say. We must all agree that he led his little expedition into . . . into . . .

JOHN PAI

> Into the Valley of the Shadow of Death. An *expedition*, as you say, I like that. Yes, they were a war party of the Rabbit Society, a children's crusade. It is so.

WHERRITT

> Peril and destruction. Even Emdotah agrees with that. But to me Sailor was not responsible. Even when he stripped the little ones of their clothing, stole it, I am convinced that he was acting entirely out of fear and desperation. He simply couldn't help himself. He was afraid.

JOHN PAI

> Fear is a disability.

WHERRITT

> It is very important to me that you understand how sorry and sympathetic I am and that you tell your people. Very important.

JOHN PAI

> I think I have it, Mr. Wherritt. Mr. Wherritt is a very sorry man.

Wherritt is done in. He has broken out in a cold sweat. He turns helplessly to Gregory.

WHERRITT

> (*confidentially*) Mr. Gregory, I've been meaning to talk to you. I should like to request a very short leave of absence, sick leave, actually. I haven't been myself lately.

GREGORY

> Yes, this dreadful weather. The Great Plains of the North American Continent. Yes, you don't look at all well, Barton. Best to look after yourself. Come along now. There are forms to fill out.

Exit Wherritt and Gregory. There is a moment in which Carrie rearranges herself, sets herself to be at her best for John Pai.

CARRIE

Oh, don't mind them, John. Let's be cheerful your last days here. Look, I've brought you something.

Carrie goes to the desk, takes up the package, hands it to him. He unwraps the gaming wheel and stick. He is not surprised, but he is moved. He handles it with care and respect. And for a moment he regards the suspended medicine wheel, backstage.

JOHN PAI

(softly) Thank you.

CARRIE

I thought you might like to have it; to take it with you. Perhaps it will remind you of home. . . .

JOHN PAI

Home? Yes, ma' am, and it will remind me of you—and of Seta, who made it. Thank you.

CARRIE

Oh, John, those poor boys . . .

JOHN PAI

The indolent boys.

CARRIE

What?

JOHN PAI

Mr. Wherritt has used the word "indolent" in speaking of the children. It means insensitive to pain, slow to develop, indulging in ease, lazy.

CARRIE

These last days have been so dreary! I wanted to be carefree and cheerful when you left, happy for you. It was to be such a special occasion, something that you would remember happily, always. *(pause)*

But there is such a pall over the school now. I cry in the nights.

John Pai, the wheel and stick in one hand, takes up a piece of chalk and writes on the chalkboard these names:

Matthew		Sailor
Mark	John	Arch
Luke		Jack

CARRIE

(continuing as John Pai writes) You know, it's silly, but I can't get last spring's picnic out of my mind. It was just one of those times, like a special afternoon out of the distant past, out of childhood, you know? There are wonderful moments, not many, but a few, maybe only one or two, but they hold you up in your life, no matter what happens to you. That day of the picnic was such a moment for me. The air was so clear and bright over the river and the trees, fragrant and deep. The plain was green, and there were vast patches of wildflowers, red and blue and white and yellow. And you and Sailor were running after the rolling wheel, and you were . . . you were, well, you were young men running, and you had taken off your shirts—against the rules—and your bodies were young and hard, and, I don't know—rippling—and you were yelling and laughing, as if that were the only afternoon in the history of time, and you were more alive than you had ever been, and I was somehow a girl again, and there was in you a wildness, a kind of life that I had never seen, never imagined, and there was in me a terrible, shining, exciting gladness, and I was somehow a girl again, and there was in me a goodness, a rapture, something worth saving for its own sake. It was, yes, rapture.

(She turns to John Pai. He has moved the point of the stick over the names; it rests on "John.") John, what are you doing?

JOHN PAI

I am counting coup.

Blackout.

ACT TWO

Scene Three

Snow falling stage left. Flute and voices echoing. Children are still until action begins, then attend closely. Spot on John Pai, asleep in chair, the three forms in a row on floor wrapped in old canvas blankets, like mummies. Mother Goodeye moves slowly into spot and stands over the forms. Emdotah moves slowly into spot and stands over the forms. He is in Kiowa dress—moccasins, leggings, a Ghost Dance shirt. There are eagle feathers in his hair, his braids are wrapped in otter skin, and his face is painted. After a long moment he falls to his knees beside the largest form and emits terrible sobs of grief that make his whole body quake. At the same time he draws a knife violently from his belt and cuts off the braid on the right side of his head. In the process he cuts his ear. He is utterly careless of the wound and the blood that rises from it. He places the braid on the largest form. Then slowly he regains his composure and stands.

MOTHER GOODEYE
>   If they are not here, then, surely, neither are we.

EMDOTAH
>   My son is here.
>>   *(singing in Kiowa)* The enemy held him, he broke away,
>>   The enemy shamed him, he made a song.
>>   Death sang with him. Warriors sing and die.

John Pai in his sleep, translates the song. Then there is the flute.

EMDOTAH
>   Haw! We are a tribe of dreamers. When I was a young man I dreamed, and I remember my dreams. You who are about me dream. It is good. Let us dream our shields. Let us dream each other, and let us dwell in our dreams. Let us dream our story, and let us be whole and honorable and true to our dream, and ourselves in it. That is how we *Gaigwu* must earn the end; that is how to be worthy of our death. We must be true to ourselves and to the story which tells of us.

MOTHER GOODEYE

The Kiowas came into the world through a hollow log. They called themselves *Kwuda*, "coming out," and it is a good name, a fitting name. There is no being without names.

EMDOTAH

His name was Seta. Set, the bear, was in his name, as it was in the name of Set-angia, whom my son called *Kon*, Grandfather.

JOHN PAI

Matthew, Mark, Luke, John, Mosatse, Koi-khan-hodle, Seta, Set-angia.

> (*singing*) The enemy held him, he broke away,
> The enemy shamed him, he made his song.
> Death sang with him. Warriors sing and die.

MOTHER GOODEYE

Seta. Bear. It was a long time ago, when dogs could talk. The people were coming out, and they were camping in the long grass, and there were dogs in the long grass, dogs dragging travois, and in the long grass there were buffalo, as many buffalo as there were stars in the sky, so it seemed, and one day there were horses, big dogs, in the long grass.

JOHN PAI

Seta. Bear. Dogs. Big dogs with hooves, dragging travois. Buffalo, big dogs with horns and hooves, dogs of the sun, Sun Dance dogs.

EMDOTAH

Crazy dogs. Dog soldiers. Set-angia, the leader of the *Kaitsenko*, the crazy dogs, the dog soldiers. They were ten men only, the ten most brave.

MOTHER GOODEYE

Each of the *Kaitsenko* warriors wore a sash that trailed the ground, and each carried a sacred arrow. In time of battle he must, by means of the sacred arrow, impale his sash in the ground, and he must stand his ground to the death.

JOHN PAI

At the Kiowa Boarding School they called him Sailor. But I tell you, he was Seta, son of Emdotah, named for Set-angia, Chief of the Crazy Dogs, Chief of the *Kaitsenko*.

EMDOTAH

My son, Seta, closely resembled Set-angia.

MOTHER GOODEYE

The thin faces, the long, narrow eyes, the long hands and feet,
white hair. Oh the resemblance was remarkable. *Eh, neh neh
neh!*

JOHN PAI

Seta, son of Emdotah, named for Set-angia, was an arrow-
maker, a maker of wheels.

EMDOTAH

Set-angia, too, had a favorite son. His son was killed in Texas.
When Set-angia heard of it, he went there and gathered up the
bones of his son. And thereafter, when he went out, he led a
hunting horse which bore the bones of his son on its back. And
at night he placed the bones in a small, ceremonial tepee, and
he said to the coming-out people, "Come, my son is at home
tonight. Come and visit him! Come and pay your respects!"

John Pai opens his eyes, stands, steps close to the bundles.

JOHN PAI

Seta, I have come to pay my respects.

MOTHER GOODEYE

Seta, son of Emdotah, I have come to pay my respects.

EMDOTAH

(*his voice breaking*) Set-angia is dead. My son is dead. I cannot
gather up the bones of my son! I am not a warrior! I am a
coward!

JOHN PAI

Seta, they say shameful things about you. They say that you
were to blame for your death and the deaths of Mosatse and
Koi-khan-hodle. They say that you were a coward.

Flute and voices echoing. The children become extremely anxious.

EMDOTAH

(*straining to hear*) Do you hear?

MOTHER GOODEYE

I hear.

JOHN PAI

I hear. What is it?

MOTHER GOODEYE

I hear. What is it? Emdotah, tell us, what is it?

The flute, voices echoing, the wind.

EMDOTAH

They are far to the south and west, and they are cold and hungry. The snow has fallen all day. It is night, and there is the freezing cold that follows such a snow.

JOHN PAI

It is clear, perhaps.

EMDOTAH

The stars are so bright that the snow shines like a fog, like a great cloud.

JOHN PAI

There are shadows, perhaps.

EMDOTAH

It is a place of shapes and shadows, a holy place.

JOHN PAI

They are camping, perhaps.

MOTHER GOODEYE

They are homesick, they are going to the camps, they are camping.

The children weep in silence.

EMDOTAH

Mosatse first. He does not fall. He kneels and folds upon himself, without words. Koi-khan-hodle, without words, moves on, for his whole strength is now in the taking of his last steps. My son, Seta, is twice as strong as the others. He could be far ahead, out of danger, but he has kept to the slower pace of the children. He cradles Mosatse in his arms, being brave for him in death. He removes the uniform and ties it round the small body in a dignified manner, like a coup string, like the captured possessions of a strong enemy. Then, farther on, Koi-khan-hodle bends and dies. My son removes the uni-form, tears it, defiles it with dirt and mud, and puts it on like a trophy, as if it were the war shirt of a best enemy. And then, stiffening, the words like twigs and dead leaves in his mouth, he taunts the night and the death that are upon him. "Come," he says, beckoning, "come on! I have no shield and no weap-ons, but I have the name of the bear, and I have words of scorn and shame to heap upon you. *Haw!* I sing my death song: I am ashamed for you. You killed my brothers so easily, without sorrow, without asking their forgiveness, and now you would kill me without honor or dignity or sorrow. Shame! You do not beg my forgiveness. But, *haw!* I forgive you and make you ashamed. You are forgiven!"—And my son lies down and dies in the snow.

JOHN PAI

He had no shield.

EMDOTAH

He had a song at last, a death song, the song of a warrior. His song was his shield.

JOHN PAI

There was no glory in his dying.

EMDOTAH

He earned his death. That is a better thing than glory.

JOHN PAI

You are wearing your hair in the old way.

EMDOTAH

Haw!

MOTHER GOODEYE

Eh neh neh neh!

Blackout.

ACT TWO

Scene Four

A day later, morning

The wheel. Lights up on classroom. It has been upset, chairs overturned, windows broken, books torn and scattered, etc. The children are conspicuously absent. Gregory stands huddled in a corner. He has been beaten. There are bruises about his eyes and mouth. He holds one hand at a curious angle to his chest, as if it might be sprained or broken. His jacket and shirt are torn. Carrie enters. She is excited. She babbles without taking close notice of him.

CARRIE

Have you seen them—the Kiowas? My God, some of them are still milling around the Agency!—raising dust and shouting, breaking things up, oh, it's, it's *wonderful!* We are quite under siege! Oh, I've never seen anything like it. Maybe they will take captives. Do you know that danger tastes something like cracklin' cornbread? *(Suddenly she is aware of the disarray, then of Gregory.)* What's happened here? Oh, my God! Oh, Mr. Gregory, George, look at you! My God! My God!

GREGORY

The Kiowa Boarding School was attacked, Carrie, *attacked,* and its superintendent assaulted. I was assaulted and wounded, as you can plainly see. Had I not resisted with my whole strength and courage, I would most certainly have been slain.

CARRIE

So it did come to violence. I didn't know. I was at the Agency, and it was so exciting! No one there was assaulted, I think. There was just a lot of shouting and confusion and commotion and . . . and color! It was mighty like a picnic! I swear it was! *(slightly more calm)* Oh, but George, you must have been terribly frightened!

GREGORY

You say they are still out there?

CARRIE

About the Agency. But they are not so angry as they were. They seem to have quieted down a good deal. Agent Adams was quite relieved, as you may imagine. He believes that war has been averted.

GREGORY

Well, truth to tell, I was not *frightened*, exactly. Say, rather, *attentive*, alert. I was on duty at my post. I was not about to turn tail and run, oh, not I. One, if not two or three—it was so sudden and chaotic—jumped me, took me by surprise, had *total* advantage of me. Treacherous, *treacherous!* That is their way, you know. I simply followed the rules. I fought back, of course, and of course they beat a fast retreat. Oh, I don't mean to suggest that I behaved with any sort of unusual courage. I kept my head, that's all.

CARRIE

To think, you might have been killed!

GREGORY

Why, yes, I dare say. You don't think of that really, in the breach. You do what you have to do, it's that simple. You do your duty.

CARRIE

You know, when Barton and I were talking, we said something about reprisal. I can't help thinking of that now.

GREGORY

Certainly reprisal had a great deal to do with it. The savages were bent on revenge; they were out to annihilate us, nothing less. They had to be stood up to, Carrie, and I stood up to them. I . . .

CARRIE

They must have been looking for Barton. What happened to him? Is he all right?

GREGORY

Barton? Oh, yes, Wherritt. *(pause, sadly)*

Well, Carrie, I'm sorry to say that Barton conducted himself with something less than heroism. He was, in fact, terrified.

CARRIE

I knew it.

Gregory points to the ceiling.

GREGORY

There, up there, Carrie.

CARRIE

> (looking) What?

GREGORY

> He hid up there.

CARRIE

> (incredulous) He hid up there? Barton? On the upper level?

GREGORY

> In the rafters, Carrie, in the rafters. Our teacher and discipli-
> narian hid among the rafters while I faced the heathen horde. I
> don't mind telling you, Carrie, I was, well, I was, ah, disap-
> pointed. Sterner stuff, and all that. It's a good thing that I didn't
> really count on Wherritt, you know?—or upon anyone else, for
> that matter. Early in the game I learned not to depend on
> others. My father used to say, "Thy hand to plant, thy hand to
> harvest." I think it's in the Bible. Anyway, Barton's gone from
> his perch. It's the damnedest thing. He's not up there now. I've
> searched. Frankly, Carrie, I think he has run away.

CARRIE

> Dear God, not yet another runaway.
>
> We're building quite a reputation, aren't we? Those poor,
> dead boys, and now Barton, and John Pai gone too. Well, it's
> just you and me, Mr. Gregory. We are what's left. We are the
> Kiowa Boarding School. How shall we endure?

GREGORY

> Oh, admirably, Carrie, admirably. Our work will go on, and we
> shall perform in the best traditions of the boarding school
> system.

CARRIE

> Will the Kiowas send their children to us now?

GREGORY

> But certainly. There is no question. This matter has been set-
> tled once and for all, with common sense and diplomacy.
> Whatever its cost to me personally. (He examines, making a show
> of, his injured arm.) It was eminently worth the sacrifice. As to
> the Indians and their disposition, I trust with Agent Adams
> that this unpleasant matter will grow out of their minds, if not
> their hearts.

CARRIE

> If not their hearts. (pause)

Speaking of the children, how are they taking this? Where are they?

GREGORY

Eh?

CARRIE

The children.

GREGORY

What? What children?—Oh, the children, the schoolchildren! Yes, of course. They are fine. Indeed. They are taking all of this, this disruption, like little soldiers, exactly, like troopers! Little troopers. Little scouts!

The children enter, take their seats, attend. Enter John Pai with suitcase, unobserved. He stands at attention, in his uniform, like a statue.

GREGORY

The children, Carrie, the children! *The children* are what we are about at the Kiowa Boarding School! Let's not forget that. We must save the children, rescue them, by God! We must save them for a life of activity and usefulness. We must save them from a life of sloth, from a life of indolence. *(pause)*

It hasn't all been failure, you know. We have had our moments.

CARRIE

Yes, we have, Mr. Gregory. Yes, we have. John Pai is our triumph.

GREGORY

(confidentially) You know, we must take advantage of that.

CARRIE

Take advantage?

GREGORY

Of John Pai's success, which is ours, rightfully: Let's admit it. John Pai is the proof of the pudding. He is the personification of our mission, don't you see? When Richard Henry Pratt set up his great experiment at Fort Marion, and when he established his school at Carlisle, Pennsylvania, his vision was that of a young man like John Pai, *exactly* like John Pai. John Pai is the problem, the reckoning, and, above all, the solution. We have a hundred Indian children at various stages of, of evolution. Their knees and elbows are black, they have lice in their hair, they speak a language that is remote and rudimentary, not to say unmelodious. *(pause)*

They peer at us as if *we* were the freaks. They look at us as if they see into us, through us. But the great truth is, Carrie, that anyone of them could become a John Pai if we just followed the formula, minded the rules. Isn't that so? Was it so obvious with John Pai?

CARRIE

I suppose not. He came well before my time, but I imagine that he came with lice in his hair and a runny nose and running sores. That's pretty much tuition here, isn't it? *(pause)*

Did you know that he had run away?

GREGORY

What? Ha! You see? Well, I need to check my records, of course —but, you see, to us accrues the credit! We have graduated John Pai. We have realized Mr. Pratt's dream. We have taken our place in the hierarchy. We are the model now.

CARRIE

Have we killed the Indian and saved the man?

(*John Pai steps forward.*)

John! Hello.

GREGORY

John, yes, hello! We were just now speaking of you. Are you off? Are you then off to the wars?

JOHN PAI

In a manner of speaking, sir. The Holy Wars. The Children's Crusade, perhaps.

GREGORY

Oh, that's quite wonderful! You are a triumph of the Christian faith, John. You will carry our banner abroad?

JOHN PAI

The Kiowa Boarding School, Anadarko, Oklahoma.

GREGORY

That's it, that's the spirit! *(pause)*

John . . . thanks. Just thanks. And goodbye. You've been, well, you've just been . . . our favorite! Our success!

JOHN PAI

You're welcome, Mr. Gregory. Goodbye.

Gregory fidgets, exits.

CARRIE

I miss you already.

JOHN PAI

It's a large thing, taking leave. I know about that.

CARRIE

It's time, isn't it?

JOHN PAI

It's time.

CARRIE

Maybe you will feel like writing to me, after a time.

JOHN PAI

Do you know, Miss Carrie, that my grandmother was a captive?

CARRIE

Is it an omen?

JOHN PAI

Don't be impertinent.

CARRIE

A picnic, John Pai.

JOHN PAI

A picnic, Miss Carrie. I'll bring the wheel.

Blackout.

END OF ACT TWO

EPILOGUE

Flute. Children in dim light. Mother Goodeye in spot stage left.

MOTHER GOODEYE

Those poor boys, the frozen boys. There was such sorrow, such anger in the camps, and it was all of no use. I was sick with grief, and then I was sick with anger, and then I was sick with hopelessness. I wanted to kill Barton Wherritt, and I took my best knife—the one I used to cut off these fingers—and I went to the school to kill him. Oh, I was looking forward to it! But, I couldn't find him, you see. Later we heard that he hid in the rafters of the school. What kind of name is *rafters*? And then he ran away. No one saw him after that. Just as well, you see. Superintendent did not fare so well. He was found and beaten up. But later it was decided among our chiefs that he was not so much to blame, and so, you see, the man who beat him up had to give him a horse. *Eh neh neh neh!* (*She dances around her cane, cackling. Pause.*) John Pai . . .

(*Enter Gregory stage left and Carrie stage right. They stand in dim light and repeat the name John Pai.*)

John Pai did not like the train. He ran away to the camps.

GREGORY

(*dumbfounded*) He what? He ran away to the camps. *John Pai!*

CARRIE

(*elated*) John Pai!

Gregory and Carrie stand in dejection and elation, respectively.

MOTHER GOODEYE

The poor boys, our hearts were broken. And the next year an even more terrible thing happened at the Kiowa Boarding School. Some of the children got sick with measles . . . (*The children turn to the audience. They are covered with red spots.*) Superintendent did not want them in the school, and he sent them home to the camps. And there the disease ran wild. The coming-out people did not know how to treat the measles, you see, and they tried to wash the red spots off. They poured buckets of cold water over the sick children, or they dipped their burning bodies in the river. More than three hundred children died. Everywhere were people grieving. Along every path were men and women, their hair cut short, or their arms and legs gashed, or the stumps of their fingers bleeding, and there were pitiful cries all around. And everywhere there were fresh graves, and at every grave were placed goods— toys and dresses and cradle boards—and sometimes a horse was killed at the grave. (pause)

The three schoolboys were taken in a wagon to be buried. Everyone was crying. And then a strange thing happened, one of those things that are so unexpected and so deep in the center of life that they become part of the story, you see. (pause)

Luther Samaunt drove the wagon, and he was a dignified man. He was wearing an army coat, one of those big, blue coats with two rows of big, brass buttons. Somehow, when he was getting down from the wagon, the brake handle got up inside the back of his coat, and Luther hung dangling there, his feet well above the ground, his arms and legs thrashing. Well, it was an astonishing sight! They couldn't get him down until someone cut off the brass buttons, and then he fell on his ass like a sack of corn. And everyone laughed. (pause)

There was crying, you see, and then there was laughter. And one was not greater than the other, neither more unaccountable or appropriate. When I think about it, you see, I believe it is a matter of balance. Even the stars are balanced, you see, and when they stray or fall, it is all right, for they will seek and find their balance in the great wheels of light. Well, for us, in the camps, that is how to think of the world; eh neh neh neh!

She dances once around her stick, cackling. The children mimic her. Flute. As spot fades on Mother Goodeye, the wheel becomes brighter.

Blackout.

END OF PLAY

Children of the Sun

The Talyi-dai, by N. Scott Momaday, 2007. Acrylic on paper. 12 × 16 inches.

To the children, including my grandmother,
of the Rainy Mountain Boarding School
1893–1920

ABOUT THE PLAY

Children of the Sun is a play written primarily for children. The principles of performance, therefore, should be wonder, delight, beauty, and fantasy, those things that especially appeal to the imagination of children. Moreover, the play is informed with spirit. It tells a sacred story, a story of the sacred. This, too, in the world of the American Indian, is a matter of the greatest importance to children, for in that world children are considered sacred beings. The story is based upon an ancient Kiowa narrative—probably a unified series of episodes (each one a story in itself) such as we call epic, although we have only a part of the original—about twin heroes. The twins are the children of an earthly mother and the god who is the Sun, and through them the Kiowas are related to the deity of the *Ka'do*, or Sun Dance. The twins are called *Talyi-dai*, "boy medicine," or "half-boys." They survive as medicine bundles in the Kiowa tribe, and they are greatly revered to this day.

Here is a dimension of timelessness, as in a creation story. The set is simple but colorful, in some sense a playground. There is a central tree, a bush to one side, two or three tepees. There is an undefined space, a no man's land, in which anything might happen. This is Grandmother Spider's place, a kind of podium from which she sings, prays, tells stories, mimes. There is sometimes a web across it. There might be projected on a backdrop symbolic drawings such as children make—wheels, suns, tepees, animals, and the like. There is the music of flutes and drums.

The story within the story of Aila, who brings color to the world, was first recorded by my daughter Cael for her first child. The play is therefore a father-daughter collaboration.

PERFORMANCE HISTORY

Children of the Sun was commissioned by the John F. Kennedy Center for the Performing Arts. The play's world premiere was presented March 4–20, 1997, at the Kennedy Center Theater Lab. Stuart Bird portrayed the roles of Aila's father, Red Bird, and First Twin. Royana Black played Aila's mother, Aila, and Second Twin. Grandmother Spider was portrayed by Cordis Heard. R. Carlos Nakai composed the music, and Meir Z. Ribalow directed the production.

A staging of the play with choreographed dance was presented by the Barter Theatre, the State Theatre of Virginia, Abingdon. Directed by Katy Brown, the production ran from March 21 to May 21, 2000, and featured Virginia Wing as Grandmother Spider; Kalani Queypo and Shammen McCune in the other male and female roles, respectively; and Susanne Trani and Derrick Alipio as dancers.

Cast of Barter Theatre's 2000 production of *Children of the Son*. *Top row* (l. to r.): Kalani Queypo, Shammen McCune, Derrick Alipio. *Bottom row:* Susanne Trani, Virginia Wing. Photograph by Ivan Scott, courtesy of the author.

CHARACTERS

THE TWINS, two boys, look-alikes, who can appear to be any age between eight and eighteen.

AILA, their mother, the young woman who marries THE SUN. She mimes a baby; otherwise she is a young woman of marriageable age.

GRANDMOTHER SPIDER, an old, spidery woman, crotchety, clownish, and wise.

THE SUN, himself, a god, a young man.

AILA'S PARENTS, whom we encounter only as a MAN'S VOICE and a WOMAN'S VOICE, introduced by GRANDMOTHER SPIDER.

AILA can play the part of the SECOND TWIN.

THE SUN can play the part of the FIRST TWIN as a grown man.

AILA or one of THE TWINS can play the part of the little boy who appears in scenes VI and XII.

Scene One
The Sun Will Do Her Such Good

The curtain comes up on a Kiowa camp at early morning. There is a large, central tree, with tepees about, one of them prominent. There are sounds of birds and activity, the Kiowa language. The form of a giant spider appears in the indefinite light at the back of the stage. Grandmother Spider appears.

GRANDMOTHER SPIDER

> Crangie, crangie, spit and spangie,
> Coola, coola, coola, coo,
> Windy, windy, cold and sandy,
> Blowtha, blowtha, blowtha, BOO!

Eh neh neh neh. Listen, children. I will tell you a story. Akeah-de. They were camping. It happened a very long time ago, when dogs could talk. (And you and I know, they still do. Why, this very morning my, little dog Sim-sim said to me . . . oh, but that is another story, don't you know? Tell it to you sometime). Well, there was a handsome couple . . .

WOMAN'S VOICE

a young man

MAN'S VOICE

and his wife. The wife gave birth to a beautiful child,

WOMAN'S VOICE

a girl child whose skin was very clear and whose eyes were very bright.

WOMAN'S AND MAN'S VOICES

She was the most beautiful child in the camp.

GRANDMOTHER SPIDER

Never had they seen such a perfect child, and she was their very own! Of course they wanted to protect her from all harm,

WOMAN'S, MAN'S VOICES, GRANDMOTHER SPIDER

and so they watched over her all the time.

GRANDMOTHER SPIDER

Maybe they were *too* watchful, *too* careful, *too* protective. Why, the poor little thing was all bundled up, strapped in her cradle,

80

kept indoors—held captive, in a way, a kind of prisoner. Well, that is why I went to see them.

Grandmother Spider makes her spidery way to the prominent tepee, stands listening to the voices inside.

MAN'S VOICE

She is such a darling. So sweet she is!

WOMAN'S VOICE

So sweet.

MAN'S VOICE

I think that she is you, your image. She will become the woman you are.

WOMAN'S VOICE

Look, her hair is as black as yours. Look, her fingers are long like yours.

MAN'S VOICE

I never knew how to be happy until you became my wife. And now you have presented me with this precious child, our daughter! Oh, my life is rich beyond my imagining.

WOMAN'S VOICE

And mine.

GRANDMOTHER SPIDER

(to audience) Well, this is a kind of yuckiness, isn't it? I mean, lovey-dovey, sweetsie-neatsie, cutesie, tootsie. Eck! Let's get on with it, shall we? *(to tepee, inside)* Hallo.
(Grandmother Spider angles her way to the opening of the prominent tepee. She raises flap and looks in.)
Oh, my sweet little darling!

Baby squeals, gurgles.

WOMAN'S VOICE

See, she knows you, grandmother.

GRANDMOTHER SPIDER

Of course she does. She is my darling, my favorite.

MAN'S VOICE

You are good with her, grandmother. You are as careful with her as we are, I think.

WOMAN'S VOICE

Yes, it is true, grandmother.

GRANDMOTHER SPIDER

Yes, yes, yes! She is yours, but she is mine, too! And now you must let me take her for a walk.

WOMAN'S AND MAN'S VOICES

Oh, I don't know . . .

GRANDMOTHER SPIDER

Eh neh neh neh. It will do her such good! The sun is warm, the air sparkles! There are puppies romping in the grass and birds singing!

MAN'S VOICE

It *is* a beautiful day!

WOMAN'S VOICE

Our darling must breathe the fresh air.

MAN'S VOICE

There is a fragrance of buckwheat . . .

WOMAN'S VOICE

and laurel.

WOMAN'S AND MAN'S VOICES

The sun will do her such good.

GRANDMOTHER SPIDER

And, little one, there are *children!* Oh, they have been asking to see you, don't you know? They will make such a fuss over you. "Where is our little bunny rabbit?" they say. "Where is our baby sister?" Oh, you will like them, my precious. You will see that there are other little bunny rabbits in the world. *(to parents)* Do let me take her for a while.

WOMAN'S AND MAN'S VOICES

Well . . . perhaps for a little while. But you must watch over her. You must not let her out of your sight.

Scene Two
Such a Bird As You Have Never Seen

GRANDMOTHER SPIDER

> Hearsay, hearsay, dogs and deer say,
> Gossip, gossip, in the noonday,
> Crangie, crangie, hobble and hop,
> Dogspeak, dogspeak, gossip must STOP!

The camp. Midday. Grandmother Spider makes her way to the tree, carrying the child in her cradle. She places the cradle in the lowest fork of the tree.

GRANDMOTHER SPIDER

> And then a strange thing happened. A beautiful bird, such a bird as you have never seen, came among the branches. It stuttered down the limbs of the great tree, its wings whirring and whistling, and lighted upon a branch very near the child.

A brilliant red spot of light is played upon the branches of the tree. It is a redbird. It darts and flutters among the branches, settles just above the cradle, and continues to flutter, to pulse.

GRANDMOTHER SPIDER

> It isn't that I took my eyes off the child. Oh, I was very watchful, don't you know? But even as I looked directly at her, full of wonder—oh, the beautiful bird! Oh, it was a bird such as you have never seen! I was blinded by a flash of lightning!

A burst of brilliant light in the tree. When it fades, there is Aila in place of the baby. The cradle falls away. She removes strips of swaddling from her arms and steps to the ground, but she clings to the tree as if she remains in it.

Scene Three
The One Who Brings the Light

AILA

I am Aila, who brings the light. When I saw the redbird I was enchanted. Even as a baby I reached for it. And as I did so, I began to grow, very quickly, it seemed, and so did the tree. The next thing I knew, I had grown into a young woman, and the tree had grown high, high up into another world. I dreamed. And it lasted only a moment. Or it lasted across a time I cannot measure.

GRANDMOTHER SPIDER

Hearsay, hearsay, dogs and deer say.

Tell us, Aila, about your dream. Tell us in the true language of dreams. What you cannot see in your range of vision you can see in dreams.

AILA

Once I awoke from a dream, and I had a feeling of loss. I looked, but I could not find the beauty in the world around me. I closed my eyes and called back the dream. In it, I danced, laughing in a brilliantly colored place. Again I opened my eyes and realized why I carried feelings of sadness. The world I lived in while awake was made of black and white and gray.

GRANDMOTHER SPIDER

Drably, drably, drably, bleak.

Black dog, white dog, gray dog, speak!

AILA

I went to my father and asked him, "Father, why is there no color in our world? In my dreams each shell, each star, each stone has a color of its own. Why isn't this so when I am awake?"

MAN'S VOICE

Color? Child, what is color?

AILA

Oh, Father, you know what color is. It's, well, it's those things that are named red and green and yellow and blue—and so many other names—all different and beautiful.

MAN'S VOICE

Red? Green? Blue? What are these strange words that you are speaking?

AILA

(to audience) I was astonished. Could it be that my father did not know what color was? I went to my mother, but neither did she know. I asked the stars and the mountains and the breezes, but none knew. They were all content with a lovely but colorless world.

GRANDMOTHER SPIDER

Red horse, blue horse, roan horse, green,
Brown and yellow velveteen.

After that Aila slept often. She was happiest when surrounded by colors that lived only in her dreams. In her waking hours she thought only of how to bring color to the world. She journeyed through every dream, looking in the skies, on beaches, in the valleys for colors, for their place of origin.

AILA

Then one night I followed a glittering river through my dream. I followed the river through a dark valley to the foot of a tall, black mountain where the river disappeared into a cave. Inside the cave I found a bottomless pool. The pool swirled and sparkled with every imaginable color. I knew that I had found the place where colors began.

GRANDMOTHER SPIDER

Eh neh neh neh.

AILA

I went to the river and gathered enough clay to make many pots. I filled them with colors from the pool. It was hard work, but I brought all the pots of color into the world. Then came the task of spreading color through the land. I dipped my long hair in the pots and brushed it against all that I could reach. The earth began to breathe brilliant colors everywhere.

GRANDMOTHER SPIDER

She brushed gold upon the morning sky and crimson on the dusk. The deepest corners of valleys and narrow crevices in rocks and mountains she could not reach with color. These were left dark. Some things the color would not adhere to—

clouds, and the foam of the ocean waves. These were left white. She was more than pleased with the effects. She was delighted to think that the beauty she beheld in her dreams would remain when she was awake. And everyone and everything on earth shared in her delight.

Scene Four
There Are House Rules

Aila stands before the Sun. Both are radiant. They stand for a long moment in silent confrontation.

AILA

. The bird . . . where is the bird?

THE SUN

I am the bird.

AILA

You?

THE SUN

Haw. I have been watching you for a long time, *haw*, and I have thought of you every day of your journey. I have brought you here to be my wife. *Haw.*

AILA

But am I of age? Am I a marriageable woman, who yesterday was a child—an infant—when I was placed in the tree?

THE SUN

Yes, you are a marriageable woman, and indeed you are worthy. You are now the woman I will have for my wife. *Haw.* I have arranged everything, and it will be as I have arranged it. Uh, you see, I have a certain authority hereabouts.

AILA

Hereabouts?

THE SUN

Haw. The heavens, in general. I am a star, the most brilliant of all.

AILA

I am a child, scarcely more. I do not know how to behave in the presence of a star. Please excuse me.

THE SUN

Well, you needn't worry.

AILA

No?

THE SUN

Not at all. *Haw.* Though there *are* house rules.

AILA

House rules?

THE SUN

No smoking. When you go to the fridge, no drinking straight
from the milk and juice bottles. No dirty socks left in the hall.
Regular times for meals and naps—that sort of thing. *And there
is one No-No above all others,* a matter of the gravest importance.

AILA

Yes?

THE SUN

Yes. Let me be very clear. Do you see that bush over there, the
low, drab, shaggy one? It is a special thing, a pomme blanche.
It is not like other bushes in the plain.

AILA

But it is a bush, after all.

THE SUN

No. Believe me, it is a singular thing. Be very careful. Do not
touch it. Never, never touch it.

AILA

(laughing) Do not touch it? Never, never touch it?

THE SUN

That is what I said. *(The Sun steps close to her, extends his hand. She
takes it, looks into his eyes.)* Do I, the Sun, take this woman to be
my wedded wife? I do. *Haw.* Do you, Aila, take the Sun to be
your wedded husband?

AILA

I do. *Haw.*

*Grandmother Spider appears in dim light behind her web. She is nearly a
silhouette. Her body is contorted into the shape of a spider.*

GRANDMOTHER SPIDER

Aila then carried the Sun's child in her womb. This was a very
lonely time for her. The Sun went away each day, and she was
by herself. At length she gave birth. One day, when the Sun had
taken his leave, Aila walked out among the dunes and the

plants, her baby in a cradle on her back. It was a quiet time for her—and she came upon the pomme blanche, the forbidden plant. In her profound loneliness she set her hands upon it. Indeed, she tore it from the ground. Through the hole where the root had been, she could see far below the world from which she had come. There were her parents, her beloved people. Her loneliness was more than she could bear.

Scene Five
A Rage Grows Up in Him

Grandmother Spider dances slowly behind her web.

GRANDMOTHER SPIDER

> Sever, sever, none and never,
> Blowtha, blowtha, blowtha, boo,
> Now and then and ever, ever,
> Story, story, sad and true.

Aila makes a rope, don't you know?—takes her little one in a cradle board on her back and climbs down the rope through the hole where the pomme blanche has been uprooted. But when she reaches the end of the rope . . .

AILA

Oh, I am still far above the earth, far above my parents and my people! Oh, oh, oh.

GRANDMOTHER SPIDER

The Sun returns home to discover that Aila, his beloved wife, has broken his law, has broken the taboo, has laid her hands upon the forbidden bush. A rage grows up in him, and he hurls a gaming wheel down the rope. It strikes the beautiful young Aila dead.

The Sun screams.

Scene Six
He Sees His Very Own Image

An open space, a meadow. Enter Grandmother Spider and little boy. He does not see her at first. He romps and plays with the gaming wheel.

GRANDMOTHER SPIDER

> (*to audience*) Well, don't you know, somehow the little boy got safely down to the ground, and, oh, he had his father's gaming wheel! He played in the meadow. I came along and spied him.
>
> Crangie, crangie, spy, spy, spy!
>
> He was just a little thing, don't you know. Why, I couldn't tell if he was a boy or a girl. Therefore, the next time I came I brought a pretty ball and a bow and arrows, and I laid them in the grass. (*She reaches down and picks up the ball. It is shot full of arrows.*) Ha! He is a boy, I see, a little warrior, don't you know. (*She pulls an arrow from the ball and holds it out to him.*) You, there, little boy, look. Look what I have for you. I have your mighty, monster-killing arrows. You will need them, won't you—to kill all the monsters, I mean, all the awful monsters about.

The boy is very wary, and his impulse is to run, but the temptation of the arrows is too great. He moves haltingly to her. She takes him by the hand.

GRANDMOTHER SPIDER

> Gotcha! Well, I will take you home with me, little one, and I will give you good things to eat and make you handsome clothes to wear. (*confidentially*) But, don't you know, there are house rules. No smoking. No bad language. Regular times for meals and naps. That sort of thing. *And there is one No-No above all others.* It is a matter of the gravest importance. The gaming wheel—whatever you do, you must never, never throw it up into the air.
>
> (*to audience*) Well, don't you know, the first time he got the chance, he threw the wheel up, up, up. It seemed to hang for a moment, perfectly still, and then it came down, down, down,

and struck him squarely on top of the head—and clove him in
two! He turns, don't you know, and he sees his spit and image.
Crangie, crangie, coo, coo, coo! He sees his very own image.
He is, he are, identical twins!

Speckle, speckle, who will heckle?

Spit and image, in a pickle.

Eh neh neh neh!

Scene Seven
This Is Nothing but a Snake

Grandmother Spider approaches her tepee. The voices of the twins are heard inside, loud, excited, unintelligible.

GRANDMOTHER SPIDER

> Spatula, spatula, spatula, grace,
> A din in my ears, and mud on my face.
> Runcible, runcOpala, opala, what's to be seen?
> Boys! BOYS! *(She beats her walking sticks upon the tepee. The noise inside subsides.)* What is this? What is this crangie business, this awful ruckus? Are you trying to raise the dead?

FIRST TWIN'S VOICE

> Grandmother, is that you?

GRANDMOTHER SPIDER

> *Eh neh neh neh.* Of course it is I.

SECOND TWIN'S VOICE

> We have something to show you!

FIRST TWIN'S VOICE

> A surprise!

GRANDMOTHER SPIDER

> *Eh neh neh neh.* A surprise! I love surprises. What is it?

She turns to audience,

SECOND TWIN'S VOICE

> Ha! You will have to guess!

GRANDMOTHER SPIDER

> Hmmm. Is it a cloud full of rain?

TWINS' VOICES

> *(laughing)* No.

GRANDMOTHER SPIDER

> Is it a meadow full of bluebonnets?

TWINS' VOICES

> No.

93

GRANDMOTHER SPIDER

Is it a river full of catfish? Dogfish? Horsefish? Owlfish?

TWINS' VOICES

No, no, no, no. You will never guess it. You are not even close!

GRANDMOTHER SPIDER

Well, I give up. What is it, pray tell?

TWINS' VOICES

Close your eyes.

The twins come out of the tepee. First Twin carries the limp body of a large snake.

TWINS' VOICES

Now open!

Grandmother Spider opens her eyes and reels in horror.

GRANDMOTHER SPIDER

What? Oh, oh, what is this? What have you done?

FIRST TWIN

Look, grandmother. We have done a good deed. We came home and found this long fellow in our tepee.

SECOND TWIN

We killed it. It was a good deed, was it not?

Grandmother Spider begins to weep and wail.

GRANDMOTHER SPIDER

Oh, my grandsons. You have killed your grandfather.

THE TWINS

Grandfather?

GRANDMOTHER SPIDER

Yes. Just as I am the grandmother of our people, so was he the grandfather. He was the wisest among us. We depended on him for our well-being. And now, grandsons, the people will have to depend on you. Now you must be the grandfathers.

(*to audience*) And so the boy twins took their grandfather

down by the river, laid him on the bank, and covered him with leaves. The frogs and crickets made a goodbye music. It was a powerful moment for the boy twins. It was the moment in which they came of age.

Eh neh neh neh.

Scene Eight
We Were Brave, Steadfast, Generous, and Good

The Twins stand apart, facing audience. They are older.

FIRST TWIN

> We were lost in a cave where lived a giant. The giant built a great fire, and the cave began to fill with smoke. The smoke began to crawl and swirl on the ceiling. It was coming down upon us. My brother made a prayer out of magic words. He spoke the words, *thain-mom*, "above my eyes," and the smoke remained above our eyes and did not suffocate us. The giant was then afraid of my brother's power with words, and he left us and our people alone from that time on.

SECOND TWIN

> We were hunting. We looked into a valley and saw a strange sight. There were soldiers in red and blue capes, and they were mounted on horses. We had never seen horses, and we were amazed to see creatures that seemed half man, half beast. My brother fought with the leader of those soldiers and killed him. The other soldiers were afraid, and they ran, but we captured their horses. From that time, the Kiowas have had horses.

FIRST TWIN

> A very old man, named Blue Hand, lost his shield. He was made fun of, because it is a serious thing to lose one's shield. One must care for his shield as he cares for his life. My brother gave his own shield to old man Blue Hand, and in so doing he gave the old man dignity and respect.

SECOND TWIN

> There were many storms that spring. Tornados were bouncing in the plain. The old people and the children were terrified. My brother made a shelter out of boulders. It was so strong that it withstood the wind and rain, the hail and lightning, even the great, turmoiling funnels that struck down from the black clouds. The helpless among us were saved.

They face each other.

THE TWINS

We became famous among the people. We performed many good deeds. Time and again we saved our people. We the *Talyi-dai*, the boy medicine, we are the children of the Sun, and because of us, our people are the children of the Sun.

FIRST TWIN

There were good times.

SECOND TWIN

There were bad times.

FIRST TWIN

There were times when buffalo and deer and antelope were plentiful, and no one was hungry.

SECOND TWIN

There were times when buffalo and deer and antelope were scarce, and our people nearly starved.

FIRST TWIN

There were times when children played in fields of wild-flowers. They grew strong and laughed.

SECOND TWIN

There were times when children huddled in the cold. They grew weak and wept.

THE TWINS

There were good times. There were bad times. And in all of these times we were

FIRST TWIN

brave,

SECOND TWIN

steadfast,

FIRST TWIN

generous,

SECOND TWIN

and good.

FIRST TWIN

We slew giants and other enemies.

SECOND TWIN

We cared for the sick and the old. We protected the women and children.

FIRST TWIN

>We were the best hunters. We provided food enough for our people.

SECOND TWIN

>We were the best warriors. We brought glory home to our people.

FIRST TWIN

>There were good times.

SECOND TWIN

>There were bad times.

THE TWINS

>And in all of these times we were

FIRST TWIN

>brave,

SECOND TWIN

>steadfast,

FIRST TWIN

>generous,

SECOND TWIN

>and good.

Scene Nine
This Is Too Strange a Thing

Winter camp. The Twins are asleep in a tepee. (We see inside as well as outside.) Meat lies outside the door. Grandmother Spider is at her web.

GRANDMOTHER SPIDER

> Sprangle, sprangle, crangie blow,
> Wrangle, wrangle, mangy crow.
> One will wither in the snow.
> One will stay, and one will go.

It was a hard winter. The buffalo had ranged far to the south. The people were hungry.

Second Twin stirs, gets up, stretches, goes out and sees the meat and is astonished. He scrambles back inside, shakes his brother.

FIRST TWIN

> (*alarmed*) What? What is it?

SECOND TWIN

> Oh, come, my brother! Come and see! There is fresh meat outside!

FIRST TWIN

> Fresh meat? What are you talking about?

SECOND TWIN

> Come! Come!

He pulls First Twin up and out.

FIRST TWIN

> (*unbelieving*) But what . . . but how did this happen? Where did this meat come from?

SECOND TWIN

> Who knows? Who cares? I am hungry. Everyone is hungry. There is enough fresh meat to feed the camp. Let us eat, my brother, then make a feast for our people.

FIRST TWIN

Wait.

SECOND TWIN

(exasperated) Wait? What for?

FIRST TWIN

Let us think about this. It is strange.

SECOND TWIN

Oh, don't be so suspicious. We have been given help in our time of need. Don't you see? It is a gift. Perhaps it is a gift from our father, the Sun.

FIRST TWIN

It is too strange a thing. Perhaps it is a test of our strength. I believe we had better not eat this meat.

SECOND TWIN

Oh, man, me HUNGRY! Me EAT!

He takes a piece of meat and eats it. In a moment he begins to writhe and groan. His body becomes contorted. First Twin looks on, horrified.

GRANDMOTHER SPIDER

And so one of the twins was transformed. He turned into a beast with little short legs and a long tail, a water beast. Then he slithered along and disappeared in a lake, and he never was heard from again. Sometimes his brother went to the water's edge and called out. He reported the news of the day, and his voice carried on the rolling water. He told of how things were with the people.

Newsie, newsie, scram and scroosie,

Jig me, jig me, don't confuse me.

Slither, slither, hither, thither,

Fan me over with a feather.

Scene Ten
You Will Speak Your Name

First Twin sits before the fire in the tepee. He is making arrows. He is now an old man. Grandmother Spider is visible but not conspicuous in the tepee. A figure appears outside the tepee. It wears an evil mask.

GRANDMOTHER SPIDER

Do you see how he works? If an arrow is well made, it will have tooth marks upon it. That is how you know. The Kiowas made fine arrows and straightened them in their teeth. Then they drew them to the bow to see that they were straight. There was the Sun's child, grown old now. We were alone at night in his tepee. By the light of a fire he was making arrows. After a while he caught sight of something. There was a small opening in the tepee where two hides had been sewn together. Someone was there on the outside, looking in. The Sun's child went on with his work, but he said to me:

FIRST TWIN

Someone is standing outside. Do not be afraid. Let us talk easily, as of ordinary things.

GRANDMOTHER SPIDER

He took up an arrow and straightened it in his teeth; then, as it was right for him to do, he drew it to the bow and took aim, first in this direction and then in that. And all the while he was talking, as if to me. But this is how he spoke:

FIRST TWIN

I know that you are there on the outside, for I can feel your eyes upon me. If you are a Kiowa, you will understand what I am saying, and you will speak your name.

GRANDMOTHER SPIDER

But there was no answer, and the Sun's child went on in the same way, pointing the arrow all around. At last his aim fell upon the place where the enemy stood, and he let go of the string. The arrow went straight to the enemy's heart.

Eh neh neh neh.

Scene Eleven
This Is the Talyi-dai, the Boy Medicine

First Twin sits cross-legged, facing the audience. Before him in a semicircle are the Talyi-dai, the ten medicine bundles. His face is painted white.

FIRST TWIN

Haw. My time has come. My work is finished, and I must hunt the buffalo one more time. I must follow the herd to the edge of the world and beyond. I shall go now to join my mother and my brother. As you see (passes a hand over his face), I am no longer here. I am here. (Indicates bundles.)

When I was a child I divided myself in two. Now I have divided myself again. I give myself ten times to the Kiowa people. Each of these medicine bundles contains that part of me which is the blood bond between my father, the Sun, and the people, the human beings. This is the Talyi-dai, the boy medicine. In this medicine I will belong to the people forever. Haw. I have spoken.

Scene Twelve
A Long Time Ago, When Dogs Could Talk

Evening. Grandmother Spider and a small boy approach a ceremonial tepee, pause.

GRANDMOTHER SPIDER

> *Eh neh neh neh.* Look, little one. The moon, the full moon. How beautiful it is!—round, big and bright, red-orange, like a campfire among the stars. That is Aila, you know. Don't you know? The one who brought the light, who gave color to the world. She is the moon, who vies with the sun. She is softer, more beautiful to behold.

Grandmother Spider and the boy enter the tepee. A medicine bundle is suspended from the lashing of the poles. The child is timid, even afraid, in the presence of so holy a thing. After a moment of silence, they go outside.

GRANDMOTHER SPIDER

> Well, no, you must not be afraid, little one. That is the boy medicine. It is our safety and our well-being.

TWINS' VOICES

> There were good times. There were bad times. And in all of these times we were brave, steadfast, generous, and good.

FIRST TWIN'S VOICE

> We slew giants and other enemies.

SECOND TWIN'S VOICE

> We cared for the sick and the old, we protected the women and children.

FIRST TWIN'S VOICE

> We were the best hunters. We provided food enough for our people.

SECOND TWIN'S VOICE

> We were the best warriors. We brought glory home to our people.

FIRST TWIN'S VOICE

> There were good times.

SECOND TWIN'S VOICE
There were bad times.

TWINS' VOICES
And in all of these times we were

FIRST TWIN'S VOICE
brave,

SECOND TWIN'S VOICE
steadfast,

FIRST TWIN'S VOICE
generous,

SECOND TWIN'S VOICE
and good.

GRANDMOTHER SPIDER
Akeah-de. They were camping. It happened a long time ago, when dogs could talk. And as you and I know, little one, they still do. Why this very morning my little dog Sim-sim said to me . . . oh, but that is another story, don't you know? Tell it to you sometime.

Crangie, crangie, spit and spangie,
Coola, coola, coola, coo,
Windy, windy, cold and sandy,
Blowtha, blowtha, blowtha, BOO!

END OF PLAY

The Moon in Two Windows

Above: Chiricahua Apache children when they arrived at Carlisle Indian School from Fort Marion, Florida, November 4, 1886. *Below:* the same children four months later, March 1887. Courtesy of Cumberland County Historical Society, Carlisle, Pennsylvania.

To all the brave children

ABOUT THE SCREENPLAY

The Carlisle Indian Industrial School (1879–1918) at Carlisle Barracks, Pennsylvania, was the first of the U.S. government Indian boarding schools. Carlisle was a grand experiment in education, intercultural relations, and federal policy governing American Indians. The tenure of the school coincided with a time of devastation for Indian peoples. They had been utterly defeated, and they were in effect prisoners of war. The Carlisle Indian School was founded just three years after General George Armstrong Custer was killed at the Little Big Horn. Public sentiment against the Indians was extreme. Nor were the Indian wars ended. The Ghost Dance and the massacre at Wounded Knee were yet to come. The reservations were concentration camps and contagious colonies in which disease and despair were epidemic.

Against this background, Carlisle was founded by a career soldier, Richard Henry Pratt, a driven and enigmatic figure whose motto was "Kill the Indian, and save the Man." At the center of these circumstances were children, children who were forced to pass from one world to another across a cultural distance all but impossible to imagine. There were survivors, and there were casualties. All were profoundly touched by the experience. This is a part of that story.

CHARACTERS IN ORDER OF APPEARANCE

LUTHER STANDING BEAR

JIM THORPE

GLEN "POP" WARNER

DWIGHT "IKE" EISENHOWER

ARMY COACH

RICHARD HENRY PRATT

STANDING BEAR

MISS MATHER

CHIEF SPOTTED TAIL

TACKETT

ETAHDLEUH

PLENTY HORSES

STANDS LOOKING (MAGGIE)

GRAY CALF (GRASS)

POLLACK SPOTTED TAIL

MAX SPOTTED TAIL

ANNA PRATT

MASON PRATT

WHITE THUNDER (ERNEST)

GENERAL HANCOCK

SIMON MANY GOATS

STONE STANDING BEAR

DICKINSON BOY

BARBER

ORDERLY

BISHOP WHIPPLE

JOSEPH TSO-ODLE

LAME

MR. STALLWORTH

LIEUT. KINGSLY

STACY MATLOCK

SITTING BULL

I

Black screen, Indian flute.

LUTHER

(voiceover) I am a man, but I remember the child I was. I was sent away from my home to do a brave thing. I did not know what I was to do, but I prepared my heart. I was taken far away from my home, to a school in Pennsylvania. All was strange to me then. After all these years I remember how strange it was. I was afraid, but I prepared my heart to be brave.

The sound of the flute is replaced by footsteps, the sound of cleats on concrete.

Interior: Tunnel, football field, West Point. Day. It is November 9, 1912, the long-awaited football game between Army and Carlisle, to many the game that decides the national championship. Light rises, and we see the Carlisle team enter the visitors' locker room. We follow.

Interior: Visitor's locker room, West Point. Day. The faces of the players are nearly expressionless. They are serious and intent, the faces of young men going into battle. We sense that they are here not to play a game—"play" and "game" are somehow inappropriate to their purpose—but to commit a decisive act, an act of bravery, of "counting coup." They are gifted physical specimens, young men who would have been able warriors a generation earlier. Jim Thorpe is one of them. He has in the summer of this year won gold medals in both the decathlon and pentathlon at the Olympic Games in Stockholm, winning ten of fifteen events. These young men seem poised on the edge of history, about to enter into a moment of extreme exertion, a moment that will determine who and what they are. We pan their faces and come to Glen "Pop" Warner, their coach. He is a man in his prime, sturdy and handsome. He has distinguished himself as the model of a successful coach, dedicated, confident, shrewd, intensely competitive, an eminent leader of men. He knows precisely the strengths and weaknesses of his players—and those of his opponents. He can take an ordinary team and make it extraordinary. In this team he has exceptional talent across the board. And he has in Thorpe arguably the greatest athlete of the twentieth century. But he is acutely aware of the danger of overconfidence. He has come to know that his Indians have no "killer" instinct. They care more for honor and bravery than for winning.

We become aware of an old man in a corner of the room. He is discreet, unremarkable, all but invisible as he listens to Warner's pep talk. This is Richard Henry Pratt.

WARNER

Pride. Tradition. Spirit. The expectation of winning. Indeed, the absolute denial of defeat—the absolute insistence upon victory. That is Army. Today we have the honor of facing that pride, that tradition, that spirit. The Army team is formidable. It has superior size and depth. It has at least two legitimate All Americans: Lee Devore hits harder than anyone in college foot-ball. Ike Eisenhower can determine the course of a game at any time, from anywhere on the field. Army is Army. You are the Indians, and you are the enemy. Army will take no prisoners today. It will do everything it can to defeat you, physically, mentally, morally.

Interior: Home team locker room. Day. We pan the faces of the Army team. They are anxious, confident, exuberant. We hold for a moment on the face of Dwight Eisenhower. He has the look of a poster boy, clean-cut and wholesome. Over this:

WARNER

You Carlisle Indians have one thing, if that, in your favor. You have a score to settle. The gentlemen of Army are the sons of the soldiers who fought your fathers at Sand Creek, the Washita, Wounded Knee. But today they have no superiority in weapons or in numbers, and they are not taking you by surprise. Today the Army meets you on a level field, eleven men against eleven men. For you, that equality can be an advantage. Make it so.

Close on: The Army coach. He scratches with chalk on a blackboard the scores and the opponents of the undefeated Carlisle team.

ARMY COACH

Just to remind you, men, the Indians have scored nearly 400

points and have held their opponents to 50. We have our hands full today. You've all heard that Jim Thorpe is unstoppable. I would like to say, don't be afraid of him, he is only human, but be by God afraid of him. If you take your eyes off him, even for an instant, he will get past you.

Close on: Eisenhower.

EISENHOWER

(*lowly, to teammate next to him*) He is only human. He can be stopped. I'll show you.

ARMY COACH

At ease, Mr. Eisenhower. I was saying, you must respect the Indians as a team. They are well coached, fit, and full of cunning. They are elusive. Think of a few of their ancestors—Crazy Horse, Joseph, Geronimo. These men were experts in hit-and-run warfare. Don't underestimate their descendants. Let that be our first order of the day.

Interior: Visitor's locker room, West Point. Day. The Carlisle team sits/kneels with heads bowed before Pratt, who offers a prayer. He speaks slowly, in the voice of a tired old man.

PRATT

On this day, O Lord, you have blessed us with a grand mission, as Christian soldiers, to prove our worthiness on the field of battle. We ask you not for victory but for courage, not for glory but for humility, not for recognition but for honor. Thy will be done, in Jesus' name. Amen.

As Warner and the Carlisle players move in a wave past Pratt out of the locker room and into the tunnel, Thorpe lags behind. For a moment he regards Pratt, his face inscrutable. It is almost as if he wishes to speak, perhaps to pay respects, but the moment is gone, and he trots to join the team on the field. Pratt follows, bent under the burden of age, an image of solitude and loneliness.

Exterior: Football field. West Point. Day. Excitement is pervasive in the November air. Everywhere there is color and chatter, music and cheers. The sun glints on the brass instruments of the bands, and streamers and pom-poms dance in the stands.

Angle on: Luther, holding the hand of his young son, moves hesitantly in the crowd, apparently looking for someone.

LUTHER

> (*voiceover*) I first saw Captain Pratt in the autumn of 1879, when he came to the Rosebud to find children for his school. I was twelve years old. I was full of wonder and curiosity. I had never seen a white man.

There is a roar from the crowd as the game begins. Close on: Luther's son. The boy registers a look of wonder and fascination. He looks up into the sky and sees . . .

Angle on: The football in slow motion clears the horizon of spectators, trees, and buildings and is isolated in the infinite sky. It sails end-over-end in a long arc that seems to span the whole length of the field and more.

Dissolve to:

II

Exterior: Rosebud Indian Agency. Day. An arrow flutters and glides through the air in slow motion. The point is wrapped in deerskin so that it will not penetrate what it strikes. It is a gaming arrow, not a weapon. We hear the shouts and laughter of gleeful children. The arrow descends upon a rolling wheel, a gaming wheel, and knocks it flat. It is a good shot by a young boy who wants more than anything in the world to become a warrior. This ancient game is part of his preparation, his training. The boy, Luther Standing Bear, walks tall to the wheel with unhurried, nonchalant steps, as if the feat he has just performed were a routine thing, a foregone conclusion. But he can scarcely conceal his pride. His heart is beating fast. The other youngsters cheer him or, if they too aspire to be warriors, observe him sideways with envy. And there is his father, Standing Bear, a warrior and chief. He is a man of singular dignity and bearing. He takes care to stand apart, but he is very much involved; beneath his mask of mild interest there is unqualified approval. A noise in the distance distracts Luther and his father, the children. They peer into the vast, wind-scoured landscape of barren soil and sparse vegetation.

Long shot: There emerges from a cloud of dust a wagon drawn by mules.

LUTHER

> (voiceover) I think in that yonder dust I saw something like an omen, a sign that my life, and the lives of my people, would never be the same again.

The wagon approaches and rolls roughly to a stop, and Richard Henry Pratt steps down, stiff from the long, bumpy ride. With him is a sixty-three-year-old white-haired woman, Miss Mather. She strikes an outlandish figure in her Eastern garb and bonnet; her skin is even whiter than Pratt's, and she is considerably more wasted by the journey. But she puts on a brave and composed face under the dust and sweat and the strings of damp white hair. She is a teacher. She has about her the look of a missionary as well. In her stern gaze is the light of Christianity, and on her matronly shoulders the very burden of civilization. The two visitors have to be seen to be believed.

There gathers a throng of agency Indians, mostly women and children, in a general attitude of destitution—of lethargy and despair. Some of the women are pregnant, some carry babies in cradles closely, guardedly, as if these bundles were the only things between them and oblivion. Life goes on, but the atmosphere of defeat is palpable. Other Indians, including the warriors and chiefs, have begun to gather aside. They are grim and wary, stone-faced. It is impossible to know their minds. Miss Mather nods and chirps in a ridiculous attempt at diplomacy. A few of the Indians register faint amusement. Embarrassed, Pratt scowls at her. There is some apprehension in him, but he maintains a military composure. There is a long moment of suspension, in which anything might happen. Then Standing Bear motions Pratt into a large tepee, a council lodge. Miss Mather tries to enter, but Standing Bear bars her way; she must remain outside. The boy Luther is also forbidden to enter; he hastens to a small opening in the tepee and strains to see what is taking place.

Interior. Lodge. Day. Close on: Pratt. He is sallow, his features sharp and glistening with sweat. He glances nervously over his audience. Behind him are several totems—an American flag, a buffalo hide (perhaps tanned and painted, a calendar), a shield, etc. Motes of dust float in the rays of sunlight that enter the lodge through the smokehole and other openings. Otherwise the light is dim. Pratt's expression is grave but congenial. He smiles with only his mouth; it is fixed and artificial. After a long moment he trains his vision on one man in particular, a man he knows well by reputation, Chief Spotted Tail. The chief's son-in-law, Tackett, half white and half Indian, acts as interpreter.
Close on: Spotted Tail looks the part of a Lakota chief. His whole person is hard and unyielding. There is no deceit in him. His eyes are piercing, his voice full of authority. He is a man who speaks his mind under all circumstances.

SPOTTED TAIL

> We have come to know the white man. He is a thief and a liar.
> He kills the buffalo, so that we starve. He takes the land, so that
> we cannot roam and hunt. He takes gold from the ground, so
> that the earth is gutted. This is shameful. We do not want our
> children to learn the ways of shame. Now you come. You come
> to take our children. Maybe you will kill them, or maybe you
> will teach them to do shameful things.

Pratt listens with all his attention. He knows that he must show proper respect, that words, spoken words, are sacred in the Indian world. He pauses after Spotted Tail's speech, considering, digesting, weighing every syllable. He clears

his throat and begins to speak, and his whole being becomes concentrated in his
words. He suppresses his tendency to preach, to convey urgency in his tone.
Rather his manner is eloquent, to the extent that he can make it so. Much is at
stake. He gives oratory for oratory.

PRATT

> Spotted Tail, you are a great man, a great warrior, a great chief.
> I am proud to stand before you.

The chiefs and elders, some thirty or forty men, nod approval at these words.
Pratt is encouraged. Spotted Tail listens carefully for more praise. He preens,
distinguished so in the company of his peers. One or two of the others are
indifferent—or distracted: there is noise from outside, shouting, jeering, the
sound of a mob. Pratt struggles to keep his composure.

PRATT

> Everyone knows your name. Everyone, everywhere, knows the
> name of the great chief, Spotted Tail.

This elicits more muttering of agreement from the chiefs. They are a speech-
loving people. They thrive on adulation. Spotted Tail's whole demeanor seems
to soften under the weight of praise, and he is for an instant off guard. In that
opening Pratt changes the tenor of his speech.

PRATT

> But, Spotted Tail, you cannot read or write. (*The audience catches its*
> *breath. Spotted Tail stiffens and blinks.*) You cannot speak the lan-
> guage of this country. You must trust interpreters to tell you the
> meaning of the treaties you sign. Do you know whether they
> interpret rightly or not? No. But you must rely upon them, for
> you have no choice. Your words, no matter how eloquent in your
> tongue, are of no use in mine. You have said that the white man
> has lied to you and stolen your land. You have said that by
> treachery he has taken your gold from the Black Hills. Consider
> this, Spotted Tail: If your children were educated in the ways of
> the white man, they would be better able to avoid the mistakes
> of their elders. They would know for themselves what is con-
> tained in the treaties, they could determine what is best for

themselves—and for you, for all your people. Spotted Tail, I urge you, I beseech you to send your children with me to the Carlisle school, so that they may soon return to you and help you to make a better life. I have come here in peace. I have come in good faith and friendship. I have come for your children.

Spotted Tail is no longer entirely inscrutable. Pratt's argument has struck a chord in him. There are traces of anger, resentment, thoughtfulness, grudging agreement in his face. The din outside, though muffled, becomes louder. A small shadow moves across the light.

Exterior. Outside the lodge. Day. Young Luther runs about, seeking the best view of what is happening inside the lodge. He is enthralled by the white man who dares to confront his chiefs. He is excited by oratory, which is so much a part of his cultural tradition. He listens intently to hear both Pratt and Tackett.

A growing number of the Indians outside the lodge jeer, protesting Pratt's presence. Especially the women are vocal, angry, and desperate, for they sense that the well-being of their children is at issue. They are moved by a growing awareness that Pratt means to take their children from them; the children are all they have left. The situation is volatile, validated in the face of Miss Mather. She looks for all the world like a woman at the stake. The sound of the women becomes almost a wailing, a keening. We shall hear this chorus again.

Angle on: A group of children playing apart from the crowd. They are not oblivious to the melee, but neither are they caught up in it. As children they are involved in their own world.

Close on: A girl child, Gray Calf, whom we shall come to know as Grass, is isolated from the others. She plays with a doll. She is an original—impish, subdued but capable of great animation, mischief, wisdom, eccentricity, certainly drollery. She wears thick glasses, which likely were obtained from the sutler or Indian agent. They give to her an air of age, even old age. The frames are small and round, crooked on her face—Ben Franklin spectacles; the lenses are thick and smudged, magnifying her eyes grotesquely. The glasses are a definition of her unlikely persona, a kind of signature. She rocks and sings to the doll, a crude, ragged thing. She hums a lullaby and crushes chokecherries in her fingers, then she places red dots on the doll's face and arms.

Close on: Her own arms. They also are marked with red dots, the marks of measles or smallpox.

Dissolve to: Exterior. Hill top, Rosebud. Day. Standing Bear and his son stand close together, their postures informed with a certain tension, an attitude of sadness, of leave-taking.

LUTHER

>   (*voiceover*) Until that day I had known the life of an Indian child. I did not know it was a poor life, a life of hardship and misery. I knew only that I was free to run and sing and hunt, that I was alive on the living earth.

The boy clings to his father; they embrace each other as for the last time. There is a long silence, then they speak in Lakota, with English subtitles:

STANDING BEAR

>   You will do a brave thing.

LUTHER

>   Yes, my father, I will do a brave thing.

STANDING BEAR

>   (*softly, his eyes shut tight*) O my son!

Exterior. Lakota camp. Day. There is general confusion, overlain with sorrow. Here a woman wails, there a man signifies his grief by cutting his hair or scarifying himself; even the very young children seem afflicted, bewildered, even paralyzed. A woman holds up, at arm's length, as if making an offering to the sun, the frame of a cradle. She keens.

LUTHER

>   (*voiceover*) After that day some of the women made cradles. The cradles were beautiful and strong; the women set their hearts and minds to the work. The cradles were harder to make than clothing, or even shields, with intricate beadwork on soft skins and straight, lattice frames. It was their way of holding on to life, I believe. They made cradles for the unborn, who were coming into a bleak, despairing world. They were not celebrations, these things; they were prayers; they were sacred, they were medicine.

Dissolve to: Exterior. Railhead, Indian Territory. Day. There is now bustle and excitement, mixed with lethargy and despair. Children are removed from wagons and horses and placed aboard the train. It is a hectic, clamorous scene. A few of the children are curious and eager to undertake the adventure, full of excitement. Most are hesitant and fearful. The range of emotion among the parents is great—from a kind of resignation to desperation.

LUTHER

(voiceover) Always, we Indian people have loved our children above all else. I did not know it then, but I know now, that it was the most hurtful thing, the worst thing imaginable, the giving up of the children.

The young Luther is outfitted in a warrior's finery. He might well imagine that his time has come, that he has now to make his vision quest, to make the crucial passage from boyhood to manhood. He assumes an air of bravado, but beneath the show is not yet the warrior, only a confused and fearful boy.

Close on: Etahdleuh on horseback. He rides into the throng, leading a group of Kiowa children. He is in his twenties, wearing a military uniform. He cuts a dashing figure above the crowd. The horse gives him a certain heroic aspect, an attitude of nobility and chivalry. He sits the horse tall and straight, surveying the scene as if he is in control of it. He is a centaur. He is Pratt's right-hand man, having been with Pratt at Fort Marion. He is to board the train with the children. He dismounts with a flourish and hands the horse to Spotted Tail. It is clear that this is a gift, made in the traditional manner of a Plains Indian give-away, an expression of honor and generosity. It is a grand moment, breaking for a moment the solemn mood of the scene. The children, especially, are struck with wonder and admiration.

Interior. Train. Day. A carriage full of children. They are wide-eyed and breathless as the train lurches into motion. There are cries and whimpers. One child has to be restrained from jumping through an open window. Miss Mather struggles to keep some semblance of order, gaining no ground at first. The children are waving and shouting to their parents.

Close on: Luther, who sees his father. Standing Bear is shouting farewell to his son, but the screech and rattle of the train drown out his words. The train slowly outdistances the Indians on horseback. The last to be seen are Standing Bear and Spotted Tail, the latter on Etahdleuh's splendid gift horse.

Interior. Train. Night. We pan over the faces of the children. One or two are asleep. Most are open-eyed, dazed, exhausted by the events of the day. They are grim and reconciled to their fate, beyond weeping.

Close on: We hold momentarily on some of the faces, those of people we will come to know: Plenty Horses is eighteen years old, a brooding young man, physically a man, a warrior; Stands Looking, a pretty twelve-year-old girl with raven hair and large black eyes; Gray Calf (sits beside Stands Looking), who is frail and weak, her eyes closed, clutching her doll; Luther's best friend, White Thunder, a slight, gentle boy with fine hands and fine facial bones; Pollack, his brother Max, and Red Road, their sister. These are the children of Spotted Tail.

Exterior. Train, caboose platform. Day. Pratt stands, staring absently at the receding landscape. He is joined by Miss Mather.

MISS MATHER

> Do you know, you smoke too much, Mr. Pratt. *(Pratt regards her with irritation, inhales deeply of the smoke.)* Last night . . . many of the boys were smoking . . . boys under your charge, sir. All the carriages were full of smoke. The smell was . . .

PRATT

> *(cutting her off)* Where do you suppose they get the tobacco, Miss Mather?

MISS MATHER

> Why, the same place you do, surely—from the train's engineer.

PRATT

> *(smiling)* Enterprising, I should say. We must not begrudge him a small business on the side.

She is not amused.

MISS MATHER

> But it is an unwholesome business, I dare say. An unchristian business at that.

PRATT

> But, my dear Miss Mather, they have no money.

MISS MATHER

> Yes, and that makes it even more reprehensible. They barter their possessions, which must be dear to them.

PRATT

> It is a lesson in commerce, Miss Mather. They will learn thrift. But your point is well taken, Miss Mather. They must not be

seen smoking by the general public, particularly at the school. That would be entirely improper.

MISS MATHER

And is it not equally improper for you to be seen smoking? You are their example, after all.

PRATT

(somewhat flustered) That is another matter, a different matter entirely!

MISS MATHER

(smugly) Why, yes, of course it is, Mr. Pratt. Of course it is.

There is a cold silence, then Miss Mather leaves the platform. Pratt scowls and blows smoke into the wind.

Interior. Train. Day. Luther surveys the other children. They are visibly unsettled. In subtle ways they are already dividing into factions, camps within camps, based on their language groups and their degree of fear. Luther turns to the rear of the carriage as Pratt enters. Pratt is joined by Etahdleuh. Some of the boys are smoking cigarettes, including White Thunder, who coughs repeatedly. Pratt distributes tobacco from a pouch and cigarette papers. Almost all the children take the tobacco, only a few the papers.

PRATT

I have observed that many of you are as fond of smoking tobacco as I am. . . . I have used tobacco for twenty years. I have found it beneficial to my mind and nerves. It relaxes me and at the same time stimulates my brain. But in white society, there are those who disapprove of it, especially for young persons like yourselves. Therefore, there will be a rule against smoking at the school. It will be forbidden. Strictly. And those who break the rule will be punished. I too will keep the rule, to set you the proper example. Now, until we reach our destination, let us smoke as we wish and enjoy it.

Only a few roll cigarettes and light them. Luther takes a pinch of the tobacco and rubs it in his palms and on his forehead. Some of the others secrete the tobacco in their clothing. Luther goes to Gray Calf and places a pinch of tobacco in her hand. Without opening her eyes she puts the crushed leaves in a tattered little handkerchief and ties it in a knot. She clutches it to her doll.

LUTHER

(*voiceover*) Perhaps it was that, the tobacco, that first gave me to understand an important difference is our minds, the white man's and the Indian's. To Captain Pratt, tobacco was nothing more than an indulgence, something that gave him pleasure or satisfied an appetite. But to the Indian it was, and is, medicine. It has religious significance. It is an offering, a sacrifice, medicine of the spirit. Through my years at Carlisle I was to peer again and again into the chasm that lay between the world in which I was born and the world beyond.

Interior. Train. Night. Pratt and Etahdleuh stand at the rear of a carriage, apparently lost in thought, watching absently the rising of a full moon.

PRATT

You know, they are so young, and they have been so isolated. This world, my world—now your world, my friend—must seem very strange to them.

ETAHDLEUH

Yes.

PRATT

I look at them, and I can't tell what they are thinking.

ETAHDLEUH

No.

Pratt turns and nods toward a boy sitting several rows forward. It is Plenty Horses.

PRATT

That one, the older one who keeps such a silence, he is an odd one, isn't he? It is as if he sees something out there in the darkness, or looks for something.

ETAHDLEUH

He marks.

PRATT

He . . . marks? What?

ETAHDLEUH

He is marking a trail. He will remember landmarks, and he will know how to return.

PRATT

Why, why that is remarkable. Really.

ETAHDLEUH

It is what a warrior does. When he goes out he marks his way. That is only—how do you say?—common sense. It is what I did when you chained me and put me on the train to Fort Marion. I marked the way in my head, but I did not return.

PRATT

Just remarkable—but futile.

Angle on: The window, Plenty Horses' reflection in it. Beyond there are passing features in the moonlit landscape—a hill, a house, a pond, a stand of trees—all distinctive in one way or another. The reflection of the face in the window is a mask of absolute concentration. Then it turns upward and stares at the full moon.
Close on: Pratt and Etahdleuh.

ETAHDLEUH

Fu-tle. What is fu-tle?

PRATT

It means. . . well, too long a trail to mark, I'm afraid. And besides, the longing, the homesickness will end, you know. As it did for you. After a little while at Carlisle, that young man— all of these young people—will not want to go home.

ETAHDLEUH

Carlisle will be his home?—their home?

PRATT

Their Christian home, their salvation.

Close on: Plenty Horses' reflection in the window. The expression on his reflected face takes on a grave and ominous aspect, a look of pronounced apprehension. The moon has disappeared, behind clouds.
Close on: Plenty Horses. There is nearly total darkness. He can see nothing but his reflection in the window. He closes his eyes and sinks down into the winding, twisting, inexorable journey of the train through time and space. After what seems to him a long time, light again illumines the window and touches his face. He opens his eyes, visibly relieved, and begins again to study the land.

Close on: Stands Looking is composed, weary but awake. Gray Calf is slumped beside her, apparently asleep. Her hold on the doll has loosened. The little bundle of tobacco has dropped to the floor.

Exterior. Train. Day. Long shot: The train chugs its way past rows and rows of corn, fields of wheat and alfalfa. Only an occasional farmhouse or river and woods breaks the vast pattern of the landscape.

Interior. Train. Day. The children toss and squirm with discomfort in their seats. Gray Calf is sprawled beside Stands Looking. Luther is awake but seems lost in thought, daydreaming perhaps. Plenty Horses keeps his vigil, stares out the window, memorizing the landmarks.

Exterior. Train. Night. The train gradually slows, and the farms and houses are closer to each other. In a minute the train enters into clusters of buildings, a town.

Interior. Train. Night. Luther's face is pressed against the window. There are lights outside. He sees people beside the train, gathered on the platform. As Etahdleuh enters the carriage, the train jerks as the brakes are applied. The train has reached Carlisle Station. The violent motion jars everyone. Stands Looking is suddenly awake, her eyes wide and blinking. She rubs them. Then she is aghast to see that Gray Calf has fallen to the floor at her feet. The small body is still, lifeless. Stands Looking tries to scream but can only gasp. Then, in a remarkable transformation, a profound calm comes upon her, something like an infinite sorrow, and she reaches down and places the doll back in Gray Calf's lifeless hands. Then she gathers herself and goes to Etahdleuh. She whispers to him, and his face becomes ashen. He pushes her aside and goes quickly out of the carriage toward the caboose. Stands Looking then goes to Luther. He reads what has happened in her face, and he takes her in his arms as she begins to sob.

Exterior. Train, caboose platform. Night. Pratt's point of view. A good many citizens of the town have come to see the Indians. They are curious, anxious, murmuring to each other. Etahdleuh appears suddenly and speaks to Pratt. Close on: Pratt's expression is suddenly that of alarm, panic.

PRATT

What? Oh, no! My God! What must we do? (in a hoarse whisper)

Listen, we must keep our heads! My God! We must be . . .
discreet, do you hear? Good God! (*with some control now*) She
must not be seen! You must hide . . . you must remove her . . .
secretly . . . do you hear. Do you hear me? Do you understand?

*Etahdleuh does not reply. For an instant he looks hard at Pratt, then turns
abruptly and reenters the carriage.*

*Exterior. Train, night. Our point of view is from a woods on the opposite side of
the train from the station and the onlookers. We see Etahdleuh appear at an
open window. He drops Gray Calf's body, bundled in blankets, to the ground.*

*Exterior. Carlisle station. Night. From the caboose platform Pratt looks out over
the crowd as the children begin to disembark.*

PRATT

(*waving*) Hallo! Hallo! Good citizens of Carlisle, here we are!
The children are here. Here they are at last! We have come to
open the Carlisle Indian Industrial School!

*The gawking citizens hoot and whistle. Some of them emit war whoops, in the
dancing, mouth-clapping stereotype. Some throw coins, a shower of coins that
fall about the children. The gesture is probably an ill-advised attempt at
welcome, but the children are taken aback. A few, Plenty Horses in particular,
pick up coins and hurl them back. This is met with cheers of delight from the
crowd. Some of the children take cover in their blankets. Some cry. All are
confused, bewildered. In the crowd we see Anna Pratt, the captain's wife, and
his son Mason, fifteen. They make their way to Pratt, who is now shuttling
children down from the train. He is so tense and preoccupied that he scarcely
acknowledges them.*

*Exterior. Train, woods. Night. Etahdleuh moves hurriedly beside the train,
carrying a shovel. He takes up the bundle from the ground and disappears into
the woods.*

LUTHER

(*voiceover*) That was a sad thing. Some of us knew even then what
had happened, what was going on. All of us knew in time.

Perhaps it was necessary to make a secret of it. Captain Pratt no doubt thought that he was acting in the best interests of the school. Always that was his first concern. And Etahdleuh, whom I had considered a warrior, was doing what he was told to do. But from that night on, I had a different view of each man.

Exterior. Carlisle, entrance gate. Night. The children are marshaled in two files, the boys led by Pratt, the girls by Miss Mather. Numb, in a state of shock, the children walk through the big iron gate into the school grounds. Here, too, are gathered some townspeople. They are more contained than the earlier crowd, and they part to make way for the children. Nonetheless, they gawk and are intimidating. Luther glances furtively about, perhaps looking for Etahdleuh, to no avail.

Interior. Boys' dormitory. Night. Luther, Plenty Horses, White Thunder, and the other boys are herded into the cold, empty building where they must spend their first night in this forbidding new world. They are cold, hungry, and exhausted. Provisions are woefully inadequate. The meager candlelight plays eerily on the walls. The old military barracks seem haunted.

Exterior. Woods. Night. Etahdleuh quickly, quietly buries Gray Calf's body. He has carefully laid her glasses and her doll on a stone nearby. He opens the little handkerchief in which she had wrapped tobacco, and he sprinkles the tobacco on her grave. He whispers a prayer in Kiowa.

Interior. Boys' dormitory. Night. The candles have been extinguished, and there is only the October moonlight at the windows. The children huddle against the cold. Luther tries to comfort his friend White Thunder, who shivers and coughs. It is Luther's mission to be brave—to do a brave thing—but he can do nothing to relieve the despondency of this night. The awareness of Gray Calf's death has spread to all the children, and grief and terror are added to their burden. There is weeping and wailing under the blankets. There is low talk in native languages. Plenty Horses keeps to himself, sullen and wary. The sons of Spotted Tail are a camp within a camp, bolstering each other in Lakota.

Dissolve to: Interior. Pratt's bedroom. Night. Pratt stands at a mirror, removing his uniform. He is haggard, uncharacteristically silent, brooding. His wife Anna is in bed, in her bedclothes, behind him.

ANNA

Oh, poor Captain Pratt. You have had a hard journey, haven't you?

PRATT

(ignoring the question) Goddamned bureaucracy! Nothing, nothing has arrived—except that goddamned organ. An organ, for Christ's sake!—the least important of my requisitions! No beds, no bedding, no clothing, no food. And there is no heat. My God, Anna, there is no HEAT! They were driven like lambs to the slaughter into those huge empty rooms in the middle of the winter night, and there is no heat! An organ, for God's sake. I suppose someone can play "Toccata and Fugue" while my little soldiers freeze!

ANNA

How many? The children, I mean. How many?

PRATT

Eighty-two, ah, actually eighty-one. Sixty boys, and, let's see, twenty-one girls. Listen, can you see to some food tomorrow? —at least enough to revive them.

ANNA

I've already made arrangements, dear. Some of the townswomen are going to help.

PRATT

Just now they need sleep. Most of them brought blankets from home, thank God.

ANNA

The poor babies. It is a worthy thing you are doing.

PRATT

God's will.

ANNA

God's and Richard Henry Pratt's. You give so much of yourself, always.

(Pratt, in his nightshirt, gets into bed.) You are so tired, aren't you?

PRATT

Tired to the death. It comes with the campaign.

ANNA

Good night, Captain Pratt.

PRATT
>   Good night, Mrs. Pratt.

Interior. Girl's dormitory. Night. Stands Looking's beautiful face is almost serene, but just under the transparent surface is abject fear and sorrow. She lies perfectly still in the darkness, her eyes wide open, listening to the mournful whistle of a train in the distance.

Interior. Boy's dormitory. Night. Luther pulls his blanket up over his friend White Thunder, whose coughing is incessant. Luther closes his eyes, but he cannot sleep. He hears the faraway whistle of the train fade into the stillness of the night.

Dissolve to: Exterior. Bandstand, Carlisle Green. Day. Anna and others (staff and townswomen) prepare food for the children on several tables. There is chatter and laughter. The contrast from the night before is extraordinary. It is a brilliant late-autumn afternoon. This is a picnic, a social occasion, a scene full of elegance and grace. This is a Pennsylvania set piece, complete with music—or a French Impressionist painting. It is also an ironic scene because the guests of honor are urchins in braids and buckskin (or agency hand-me-downs). Not-withstanding, the mood of the children has risen sharply; there is hope.

LUTHER
>   (*voiceover*) Those first days at Carlisle were a time of coming together. We came from different places, spoke different languages, and observed different customs. But we were all Indians, and we were of one heritage. And we were young, and young people have the spirit of play, and play is a powerful bond. Play overcomes fear and uncertainty. In a little while we became one tribe, one family; we were all brothers and sisters. We might have carried one flag, one shield. Our strongest loyalty was to each other.

Some days later. Interior. Carlisle classroom. Day. Uniforms have arrived. The task of fitting them to the children is arduous, and there is much confusion. Teachers and staff unpack boxes and try to hand each student appropriate pants, jackets, shoes, etc. It is mostly guesswork, and the scene dissolves into farce. [NOTE: This scene should not be scripted in any detail but left to the imagination and discretion of the director when the time comes to piece it in.]

Interior. Carlisle classroom. Day. Girls are seated at desks. Miss Mather stands at the blackboard. On the teacher's desk are a book and papers, an inkstand. There is an American flag on a staff and on the wall portraits of George Washington and Abraham Lincoln. On the blackboard are two columns of girls' names, perhaps twenty in all. Miss Mather holds a pointer, which she raps on her desk. The girls are quiet, attentive.

MISS MATHER

> Now, students, this is what we are going to do. We are going to choose names from the board. Each one of you will choose a name, and that name will be yours from this day forward. I believe that now you know enough English to understand what I am saying, but I know that these names are new to you. They are good names, Christian names, and each one of you will be pleased to have one of these for your own, your very own. Let us begin.
>
> *(She beckons to a girl in the front row.)* Now, I believe you are Miss . . . Miss Looking, Miss Stands Looking. Please come and choose a name from the blackboard. Here, dear, you may use the pointer.

Stands Looking rises and comes forward with hesitation. She is extremely reluctant to be the object of attention. Some of the other girls giggle, but they are restrained, respectful, most of all curious. Miss Mather takes Stand Looking's hand and places the pointer in it. Then she indicates that it must be used to indicate one of the names. With hesitation, Stands Looking points to the name "Margaret."

MISS MATHER

> Good, good! Oh, very good. You have chosen a very good name indeed—Margaret. *(to class)* You see, girls, Miss Looking has chosen the name Margaret. From now on she will be Margaret Looking, ah, Margaret Stands Looking. And sometimes Margarets are called Maggie. It is a nickname. But I will explain that later. Margaret, Margaret, Maggie! Oh, splendid, splendid.
>
> *(Maggie Stands Looking returns to her seat, much relieved to be out of the limelight.)* Now, who will be next? Is there a volunteer? Raise your hand.

Close on: Gray Calf. It is unmistakably she, though she has not her glasses, and she squints to see. She is the only one not in uniform; she wears the tattered dress in which we saw her on the train. She raises her hand emphatically and walks briskly to the front. Miss Mather, though she has seen Gray Calf on the train, appears not to recognize her, but the other children react with a kind of formal silence, some bare acknowledgment of that which is beyond their understanding. They are not afraid, but they are reserved. They seem to wait for a signal to respond to her directly. Gray Calf is what the Pueblo people call a Koshare, one of the society of holy clowns, a figure both worldly and other-worldly.

Before Miss Mather can instruct her, Gray Calf takes the pointer and touches it to the name Grace. It is done with finality.

MISS MATHER

> (*nonplussed*) Oh, oh, yes I see. Well, good, you have chosen your name. Good. Good. Will you, ah, will you say your name for us, please?

Gray Calf assumes a posture, surveys the room, and cracks an exaggerated smile.

GRAY CALF
> GRASS!

It is the signal. The girls burst in laughter. They repeat aloud the name Grass until it becomes a chant: "GRASS, GRASS, GRASS!" Miss Mather tries in vain to restore order. There has entered an unaccountable presence upon the Carlisle Indian Industrial School.

LUTHER

> (*voiceover*) I don't know how it happened that Gray Calf returned to us, but it happened. Perhaps it happened because we were in need of her. We were so disheartened when she died. We were devastated. It seemed the worst possible sign, the worst possible beginning of our lives at the school. But she came back to us, and we were glad. Some things go out of our lives, but if we are no good without them, if we have great need of them, some things come back. That is how it is in our camp, in our world.

Gray Calf had gone, but Grass came to be with us. She was our little sister, and we looked out for her.

Exterior. Bandstand and green, Carlisle. Day. Pratt stands on the bandstand with General Hancock, military advisor from Washington, sent to evaluate the progress of the school. Hancock is impressive in full uniform, tall and straight, and authoritative. Pratt, too, is attired in his military best, but he hasn't Hancock's style. Moreover, he is a bit obsequious in the presence of his superior. They observe boys on the parade ground. Etahdleuh leads them in a feeble attempt at a marching performance at best. There is some snickering in the ranks, some mischief. Pratt is a bit embarrassed, and a bit put out. Hancock struggles to conceal his amusement.

Pratt steps down and inspects his soldiers. Hancock accompanies him, a step behind. This is Pratt's show.

PRATT

You are now part of the corps of cadets at the Carlisle Indian School. You are a chosen few. You have been chosen to represent the school to its advantage. You have been chosen to demonstrate to the nation and to the world my . . . our conviction that the Indian can be civilized, that he can become a responsible citizen of the United States, a productive member of society, a Christian servant of God, and a bona fide human being.

(*Pratt stands before Plenty Horses, whose long hair is loose and whose pant legs have been cut off and fashioned into leggings.*) You are forbidden to violate the uniform of the United States Army. These uniforms are to be kept clean and worn with pride. Etahdleuh, my aide-de-camp, will teach you how to keep your uniforms clean and pressed, how to keep your brass bright and your shoes polished. And you will learn to speak the English language. That is first and foremost! The languages you brought here from the wilds will be of no use to you. They are impediments to your learning. The English language will be the key to your success, your salvation. Now, men, let's hear it! How many here want to speak English? How many? HOW MANY?

Some raise their hands, some do not. Pratt is visibly disappointed and perturbed.

*Close on: Boys. Their expressions range from indifference to defiance. Pratt
continues in another voice. It is almost menacing.*

PRATT

> You will see, gentlemen, in time, in the fullness of time. Time is
> on my side—on the side of right. You will come to take me
> seriously. Believe me. *(to Etahdleuh)* Dismiss these . . . men.

Pratt turns to Hancock. There is a moment of silence.

HANCOCK

> Well . . . well. Well done, Captain. You seem to be on top of
> things here. You have your work cut out for you . . . but I'm sure
> you will succeed, the Indian school will succeed. And Carlisle
> Barracks is the right place. You have a fine facility here.

PRATT

> Thanks to you and your department, General.

HANCOCK

> After your presentation, we knew it would be a good risk. The
> odds were right.

PRATT

> The school is my life.

HANCOCK

> A worthy purpose, indeed.

*Interior. Boys' dormitory. Night. Some of the boys have formed a cadre, a kind
of camp. They gather after curfew, secretly, taking care not to be found out.
They sit round a single hooded candle. They have evolved a secret society,
complete with ritual elements. There is an opening prayer in one of their native
languages. Pollack has an eagle-bone whistle. He places one end into a vessel of
water and blows into the other. It makes the sound of a bird warbling. He blows
in each of the four directions. Then there is talk, mostly in such English as they
have, assisted by sign language.*

LUTHER

> I ask you to hear me. I have something to say. We all have
> things to say, perhaps. Some of you speak in tongues that I do
> not know, and some of you do not know my tongue, but I will

speak. Somehow we will understand each other; such things happen when there is need. I am Lakota. I am too young to speak in council, but I will speak. I have come here to do a brave thing. I want to be a warrior. My father is a chief. He is a famous man. I think we have the same wish, you and I. I think you want to do a brave thing, too. Is that not so? I believe it is so. I have spoken.

They pass a pouch of tobacco around their circle clockwise. Each one takes a pinch and rubs it on his hands and head. Luther rubs the head of Ernest White Thunder, who lies sick behind Luther outside the circle.

SIMON MANY GOATS

I am Dine, Navajo. I want to draw with colors. I don't know if that is a brave thing. My father died in the Long Walk to Bosque Redondo. My mother is a weaver. I have spoken.

PLENTY HORSES

(*in Lakota: Luther interprets*) I am Lakota. I am meant to be a warrior, but there are no warriors here. This is not a place for warriors. I will have my name, Plenty Horses, and I will have no other. The whites say they are going to cut my hair. They say they are going to make me eat boiled leaves. I will keep my long hair, and I will not eat leaves. I do not like to talk through the mouth of another. I have nothing to say.

Etahdleuh enters quickly, quietly. The boys accept him unequivocally. They regard him as one of them, but one who has seen much more of the world, who has, in effect, been on many hunts, many raids. He breaks in:

ETAHDLEUH

(*rapidly*) Come to warn you. Captain Pratt is coming. He knows this meeting. He is close behind me. Too late to hide. Stay where you are, but stand attention.

Pratt enters suddenly. He has on his sternest face. The boys are rigid.

PRATT

So. Well, well, a parley, is it?—and after hours. (*He surveys the*

scene slowly, carefully.) There is some good reason for this viola-
tion of rules, I trust.

(to Etahdleuh) I saw you come in. Had you knowledge of this?
(Etahdleuh does not answer.) I see.

(to all) It must be a secret, your meeting. And it must be a
matter of importance, the subject under discussion, for you to
have broken the rules of the school.

The silence is palpable. Pratt scans the room as if conducting an official military inspection, which in effect it becomes; he even draws from his jacket a pair
of white gloves. Something catches his eye, a beaded pouch slightly protruding
from under a bunk. An eagle feather is affixed to it. He steps smartly to it, as if
finding crucial evidence at a crime scene, but takes it up carefully, almost
gingerly, as if he is afraid that it might do him some harm.

PRATT

And what, pray tell, is this? Who might this belong to?

Pratt looks all around and waits for an answer. It does not come. In a sense, he
seems to enjoy this confrontation. It is high drama, and he is at the center of it.

PRATT

Well, bless my soul, gentlemen. We seem to have a conspiracy
in our midst.

(holding up the pouch, turning it to the light) What are the contents, I wonder. Surely they are wondrous. It is surely an exotic,
perhaps magical, thing.

Then Pratt senses that the audience slips from the palm of his hand. He has gone
too far. His sarcasm verges on desecration, perhaps sacrilege. He reverts to his
military, authoritarian form.

PRATT

(nearly shouting) Who does this belong to? Whose bunk is this?
(shouting)

I demand to know!

Now the boys are seized by fear. Silence will no longer suffice. Ernest White
Thunder, who has managed to stand at attention, steps forward, trembling.

Pratt regards him with disappointment. This boy is frail and sickly; it will not do to intimidate and bully him. He cannot be the scapegoat Pratt hoped for.

PRATT

Not yours. Yours?

ERNEST

My medicine.

A pause. No one, including Pratt, seems to know what to do next. He looks at the pouch in his hand as if it is a poisonous flower. He looks up again at Ernest.

PRATT

This, this *fetish*, it is yours, then?

ERNEST

(almost inaudibly) Yes.

Etahdleuh intervenes, fearing that Ernest might collapse.

ETAHDLEUH

It is his medicine, Captain.

PRATT

Medicine?

ETAHDLEUH

It protects him, sir.

PRATT

Protects him? Oh, yes. I have heard of this sort of thing.

Medicine. That is not a word that Indians know how to use. This is a heathen device. It has no place here. This will not protect you here at Carlisle, Mr. White Thunder. Don't you dare to call it medicine. It is a device of the devil! What's inside? What are its contents?

His voice has become shrill. Ernest cannot speak. He has begun to shake violently, his eyes to glaze. Pratt is either oblivious or insensitive to the boy's condition. Etahdleuh steps toward Pratt, who steps back, a look of disbelief on his face. The moment passes.

ETAHDLEUH

He doesn't know, Captain.

PRATT

Doesn't know . . . doesn't know?

ETAHDLEUH

His grandfather gave it to him. It is not to be opened . . . it is sacred.

PRATT *takes a deep breath, speaks slowly, evenly.*

PRATT

This, this ignorance, this superstition has no place at the school. We are soldiers of the Lord, Jesus Christ. We are civilized, enlightened, saved. When you set foot upon these grounds, you left such things as this *(holds up pouch)* behind you forever.

(To Etahdleuh) Etahdleuh, are there other such things here . . . hidden about? *(Etahdleuh looks away, says nothing.)*

I see. Etahdleuh, I want you to make a thorough search of these quarters. I want you to find every one of these pagan trappings, and I want you to get rid of them. Get rid of them at once and for all. That is an order. Is it understood? Is it?

ETAHDLEUH

(quietly) Yes, Captain.

Pratt exits.

LUTHER

(voiceover) That night we came together. Etahdleuh told us that we must give up our medicine. It was sad to do so, but we put our Indian things, our sacred objects, in a bag and gave them to him. We did not know what he would do with them, and we did not ask. I felt better toward him. I felt that night, especially, that he was trying to keep himself an Indian, trying hard, as we all were. The giving up of our sacred things was a sacrifice that made us stronger somehow.

Luther goes to Etahdleuh after the objects have been surrendered.

LUTHER

Maybe we have done a brave thing.

ETAHDLEUH

Maybe. Yes.

LUTHER

Have you seen Grass?

ETAHDLEUH

Not today.

LUTHER

You know, I thought I saw her come in the room tonight, earlier, when we were in the circle—come in and stand in the darkness for just a minute or two. And then she was gone.

ETAHDLEUH

She is everywhere, and nowhere.

LUTHER

She does not see very well, I think.

ETAHDLEUH

I know. I have her glasses. I will give them to her.

Dissolve to: Indian Field, Carlisle. Day. It is a beautiful day, sunlit, full of foliage. The field is brilliant green. There are only two people; they are walking on the field, and they are rather far away—a man and a child, holding hands. Now and then the little girl skips and hops, and we hear the faint sound of their laughter. We approach a little closer, and the little girl is in her tattered dress, and now and then the sun glints upon her glasses. They pause, and Etahdleuh takes both of Grass's hands and swings her round and round.

III

November 9, 1912. Luther and his son Stone sit in the stands amid the tumultuous crowd. Stone has a cornet, which he now and then brings to his mouth and blows a note or a bar to cheer the Indians on. They sit just above the Carlisle bench, where Pratt is seated. Stone is proficient with the cornet; the bars he plays are strong and melodic; he attracts attention. People turn and applaud him. After a particularly well-made effort, Pratt turns and looks. He is overjoyed to see Luther; his whole countenance takes on a glow. He climbs to join the two, and they make room for him. There are embraces; it is a touching reunion between the two men. The boy takes it in stride, tolerates Pratt's backslaps and effusiveness, and blows his horn.

The scoreboard reads, "Army 6, Carlisle 0."

Exterior. Football field, West Point. Day. The game is hard-fought. We can hear the crack of leather on leather even above the noise of the crowd.

Close on: Carlisle backfield, just before it runs a play. The four players are in a crouched stance, ready to spring. Their faces are dirty and grim, determined. Thorpe is at the left wing. He is bigger than the others, but less than six feet, less than 200 pounds. The ball is snapped. The Carlisle line lunges forward, smashing into the much heavier Army line. The Army line gives and breaks. Alex Arcasa darts into the hole, followed by Stansil Powell. At the same time Gus Welch races on a fake around the right end, and Thorpe follows for a step, then plunges into the opening made by Arcasa and Powell. He is already in the secondary, at full speed. Army defenders Lee Devore and Dwight Eisenhower lunge at him from either side, but he is a step beyond them when they crash into each other. Thorpe scores, and Eisenhower is carried unconscious from the field.

Angle on: Stands. A thunderous roar goes up from the Carlisle fans. Stone is beside himself with glee, excitement, triumph. He leaps into the air, nearly losing the cornet, and comes crashing down into Luther's lap. Luther and Pratt are nearly toppled, but all are upright again, hugging and cheering.

LUTHER

(voiceover) I had returned with my son from South Dakota. I felt

some need to return to the East, where I had lived such an
important part of my life. I don't know how many of us are
given the chance to return to a place, after many years, in which
their lives were changed decisively. It is a blessing, I believe. It
was for me, and I wanted my son to share in it. And Captain
Pratt had been a principle presence in my boyhood. It was
good, good to see him once more.

*Dissolve to: Exterior. Carlisle Green. Day. Luther and Ernest are walking to-
gether in the directionless manner of boys with free time. They talk and laugh,
having begun to feel more or less comfortable at the school. They come upon
Mason, who is alone near the bandstand, humming to himself and tossing a
football in his hands. He greets them.*

MASON
    Morning.
LUTHER AND ERNEST
    Morning.

Mason sees that these two are shy, but curious.

MASON
    Want to play catch?

Luther and Ernest look at each other, puzzled.

LUTHER
    What? What cat . . . caath?
MASON
    Oh, just, you know?—a game. We throw the ball back and
    forth. It's fun. Here.

*He tosses the ball to Luther, who manages to catch it in spite of his surprise.
Luther and Ernest examine the football closely, as if it might be alive. They have
never seen a football before.*

MASON
    (after some moments, gesturing) Hey, toss it back.

Luther tosses it back, awkwardly. The next toss comes to Ernest, but he drops it,
and his toss back is even more awkward. Gradually they make a game of it. We
ascend at an angle above them until they are a small cluster in a great and
beautiful field—the green and buildings of Carlisle.

Exterior. Indian Field, Carlisle. Day. Coach Warner is introducing the game of
football to some Carlisle boys. He is remarkably patient with them, but they try
him sorely.

WARNER

> Boys, I've asked these fellows to help us. They are from Dickin-
> son College, down the way. They are on the football team there.
> Now, you know a bit about the fundamentals of the game, but
> you have not had the chance to compete. We are going to have
> these fellows run some plays at you. You are going to try and
> keep them from scoring.

The teams line up, the Carlisle boys in a ragtag, tentative way. Their minds are
not on the business at hand; they are talking, laughing among themselves. The
Dickinson boys are disciplined, concentrated. The ball is snapped, and the
Dickinson ball carrier runs easily around end and straight for the goal line. One
of the Carlisle boys has a clear shot at him, lunges, brushes him, and falls
rolling on the ground, laughing. Warner picks him up in disgust and asks
gruffly, "What the hell kind of a tackle was that? What do you think you were
doing?" The boy replies, still laughing, "I was counting coup."
One of the Dickinson boys comes up to Warner.

DICKINSON BOY

> We'd sure like to help you out, Coach Warner, but I don't think
> they're ready for a scrimmage.

WARNER

> No.

DICKINSON BOY

> I understand they . . . well, they don't have football in their
> blood, I hear. None of them have ever played it before.

WARNER

> Never. Ever.

DICKINSON BOY

Well, sir, they can run like the devil, that's for sure. You can probably get a good track team together.

WARNER

We'll see.

Dissolve to: Interior classroom, Carlisle. Night. The room has been made into a makeshift barber shop. A man from the town has come to cut the boys' hair. We are back in 1879. The boys still have their reservation clothes, their long hair. The barber is at his chair, and the boys are waiting in line, dumb, frightened, as if they are going to an executioner. There is an orderly to keep the proceedings under control. Pratt's wife Anna supervises.

ANNA

(to barber) Captain Pratt has asked me to look on here. He is away until tomorrow. On business in Washington, you see.

The orderly seats the first boy in the chair, and the barber cuts his hair rapidly. The boy is rigid, tears streaming from his eyes. Anna looks on and makes cooling, soothing sounds. Her usefulness here is doubtful, but she assumes her best supervisory air and is officious. Occasionally she comments to the barber, things like, "Oh, that looks very nice," and "I wonder if you could just even it out a bid on his left side." As soon as one boy is finished, another is placed in the chair. It is an exercise in agony, a profound humiliation. We see Luther in his turn. He endures.

ORDERLY

Next to last one, sir.

BARBER

Bring him on.

The orderly takes Plenty Horses' arm and tries to move him to the chair. Plenty Horses is eighteen, strong and agile. There is danger and desperation in his face. Suddenly he pulls back violently and throws off the orderly.

PLENTY HORSES

NO!

BARBER

(alarmed) Now hold it, son!

PLENTY HORSES

    NO! You no cut my hair. NO!

The orderly grabs Plenty Horses and tries to restrain him. This is a nearly fatal mistake. Plenty Horses in an explosion of his whole body breaks the orderly's hold, whirls, and throws the orderly to the floor. In the same motion he grabs the barber's scissors and holds the points to the orderly's throat. Anna's hand flies to her mouth, and she gasps in horror. The other boys are frozen. The orderly is shaking, his eyes closed tight. Plenty Horses slowly withdraws the scissors and drops them to the floor. He steps back.

BARBER

    My God. (then *softly*) All right. All right, son. I won't cut your hair if you don't want me to. (*pause*)

      But look, all the others cooperated, even if they didn't want to, and I will have to tell Captain Pratt that you refused.

Interior. Pratt's bedroom. Night. A pale light shines through a window on the face of Anna. She is alone in bed, asleep. Suddenly the silence is broken by a piercing voice wailing. It is loud and prolonged, a deeply disturbing sound, a crying out, an unearthly lamentation. Her eyes open wide, and she springs to a sitting position. There is intense alarm and fear in her face. She creeps to the window and looks out.

Exterior. Carlisle Green. Night. Plenty Horses crouches near the bandstand in the moonlight. With a knife he cuts off his braids, wailing in grief, then the hair of his head close to his scalp.

Exterior. Girls' dormitory. Night. Grass's face in the window. She is peering out at Plenty Horses with profound concern and compassion. She begins to keen. The faces of other girls appear behind her; they cry and take up the keening. They spill out onto the porch, and the sounds grows louder. Plenty Horses' wailing and the girls' keening become one shrill, eerie chorus on the night.

Interior. Pratt's bedroom. Night. Anna looks down on the green, her expression very grave. The wailing and keening have reached a crescendo. It is unabated. She wrings her hands.

ANNA

> Oh, dear Lord, the town! The town will hear! What will they think? Oh dear, dear Lord! What will they think? Oh Captain Pratt, I wish you were here!

Exterior. Bandstand. Day. Anna with barber, orderly, several teachers and staff, and students. They stand where Plenty Horses cut his hair the night before. There is an air of perplexity and remorse about them, a quality of shame.

ANNA

> What on earth was it all about?

BARBER

> It seems, ma'am . . . I have heard, been told that long hair is sacred to them . . . especially to the warriors. And for the Sioux and the Kiowas and Cheyennes, cutting the hair signifies grief, death. I . . . well, to tell you the truth, I don't know. These people, the Indians . . . it is all beyond my understanding.

ANNA

> Yes, yes, so it is. It is quite beyond our understanding.

Grass steps forward from among the students. Like Plenty Horses she has cut her hair. It is short and ragged. She raises a tiny fist.

GRASS

> Sumbitches. You do not understand.

Dissolve to: Interior. The Old Hessian Guard House, Carlisle. Night. The guard house is a stone structure, very old but solid, pitch black inside and unheated. The iron door creaks open. In a rectangle of moonlight Etahdleuh and Luther enter. They close the door as quickly as they can. Etahdleuh strikes a match and lights the lantern he has brought with him. The room is dimly lighted, enough to see Plenty Horses sitting on the floor, his back against the wall. Etahdleuh and Luther sit down on either side of him. Luther hands him a blanket and some leftover food from the mess. They sit in silence for a time, while Plenty Horses eats. Then:

ETAHDLEUH

> (to Plenty Horses) What you did last night at the bandstand. It

was good. It was good that you cut your own hair. It was your sacrifice, and not theirs. And it was your mourning, not theirs. You were Plenty Horses. You were your own being, and not theirs. You are an Indian. Always be an Indian. That is who and what you are. That is your self, and it is the best thing you have.

LUTHER

(to *Plenty Horses*) You were brave. You did a brave thing.

(*voiceover*) We sat there on the cold floor for a long time, even after the lantern had gone out. We said nothing; there was nothing to say, but we were close together in our hearts. We had all broken the rules of the school, but it was not dishonorable. There was bravery in it—and new respect for each other.

Interior. Church, Carlisle. Day. Luther and Ernest stare at a large stained glass window; it is a scene of Calvary, Christ bleeding on the cross. It is an appalling sight to them. It is entirely outside their frame of reference, and they are repulsed by it. They proceed with others into the church. They take seats.
Bishop Whipple stands at the pulpit before his congregation of Indian schoolchildren, teachers and staff from the school, Captain and Anna Pratt, and some townspeople. He is aged and doddering, and he speaks with a lisp. His rheumy eyes burn with zeal, and he is very pale, seemingly bloodless. He is a Puritanical, humorless man. He waits while a hymn is played on the organ.

BISHOP WHIPPLE

Behold the wonders of the almighty God. He hath made the heavens and the earth. He hath made the oceans and the continents. He hath made the mountains and the rivers, the valleys and the hills. He hath made the animals and the fishes and the birds. He hath made Man. And He hath made Man in His image.

And behold his creature, Man. Man is finite, weak, and wholly unworthy. Man is a sinner! He deserves damnation. He deserves to burn in the everlasting fires of hell. BUT, BUT, BUT. He is the image of God! He can therefore be saved. You can be saved if you eschew evil, if you renounce Satan! You can be saved because you are made in the image of God!

Who among us hath seen the face of God? Who hath seen the whiteness of His glorious hair? Who hath seen the blue of

His immortal eye? Who among us hath seen the clear alabaster of his perfect brow?

You are souls who have been lost in darkness. The shadow of the heathen wilderness lies upon you. You have seen not the face of God, but the face of the savage fiend. But heed, you will come forth into the light. You will be cleansed of the squalor and misery of the wilderness, and you will be saved! You have only to accept God's mercy, which is infinite.

Exterior. Church. Day. Pratt, Anna, and Mason follow the children out of the church, greet others. Etahdleuh marshalls the boys, Miss Mather the girls. There are salutes, pleasantries. Then the family strolls on alone.

PRATT

You know, dear, Etahdleuh is a great help to me, well, to all of us, really, isn't he?

ANNA

I don't know what you would do without him.

PRATT

I have been trying to think of some way to reward his service, to let him know how much I value him—a commendation of some kind, perhaps.

ANNA

He has come to be like a member of the family. He has been like an older brother to Mason—hasn't he, Mason?

MASON

He's teaching me sign language.

Pratt pauses, looks at Mason.

PRATT

What's that, son?

MASON

Etahdleuh, he's teaching me the Indian sign language, after school . . . some words in Kiowa, too. I know how to say hello and sit down, things like that.

PRATT

(*to ANNA*) Did you know about this?

ANNA

Why, yes. I thought you did. You're not upset?

PRATT

Do you think it's appropriate?

ANNA

Good heavens, Richard. Etahdleuh has been your obedient servant and friend for years. You yourself have said that he has
been . . . saved, assimilated . . . civilized.

PRATT

Yes, so I have, and it is true. Essentially true. But I'm not talking
about his . . . assimilation, as you call it. I am talking about his
holding on to Kiowa and sign language. It goes against the
whole purpose of the school. It . . .

ANNA

I really don't see the harm in him teaching Mason a few words
in Kiowa—or signs. What's wrong with that? What if the words
were in French or German or Chinese, for that matter. What
about sign language for the deaf?

MASON

It's not as if he's trying to make an Indian out of me. And,
besides, it's fun; it's kind of like a secret language or a code.
The kids at my school don't know what to think when I make a
sign or say, "Getaig'ya." They just look, you know, confused,
and I laugh at them.

PRATT

I guess there's no harm . . . but, frankly, I'm a bit disappointed
that my aide would violate the rule of speaking English only. I
have given that man my trust.

ANNA

He is to be trusted, Richard. And our son's instincts are to be
trusted. Our son has good judgment, just like his father.

*Exterior. Grandstand and green, Carlisle, winter. Day. In their military coats
and capes, the boys march counterclockwise in a circle, inside of which the girls
march clockwise in a smaller circle. This is known as the "flirtation march,"
and it is designed to let the students encounter each other on a social basis. The
boys whistle and make innuendos; the girls giggle. Presumably some lasting
relationships will come out of these highly controlled encounters. We recognize
some of the students. It is one of the more enjoyable activities at Carlisle.*

LUTHER

>(*voiceover*) Early on, when I was made to choose my new name, I could not at first pronounce it. For nearly all of us, the "th" sound in English was nearly impossible. I remember taking the pointer from Miss Mather and pointing to "Luther" on the blackboard. I had never seen or heard the name before, but Miss Mather taught me and the others how to pronounce it. She taught us the "th" sound in a way that we would remember forever.

Interior. Classroom, Carlisle. Day. Luther points to the name.

MISS MATHER

>Ah, very good. Mr. Standing Bear has selected the name "Luther." Now, Luther, say your name for us. "Loo ther, LOO THER, LUTHER." Repeat, Luther.

Luther looks at her imploringly. He wants to please, but his tongue is tied. He makes exasperated faces. At last he produces sound.

MISS MATHER

>Uh, no. Not quite. "Loo ther. LOO THER. Let's try again."

LUTHER

>La ter, lo tare.

The other boys begin to snicker.

MISS MATHER

>All right, Luther, let's try one syllable at a time. Now, after me, LOO.

LUTHER

>LOO.

MISS MATHER

>EXCELLENT! You've got it. LOO. Oh, that's a very good boy. Half way there. Now, after me, THER.

LUTHER

>TERE . . . TARR . . . TARE.

MISS MATHER

(becoming frustrated) No, that's not it. Class, all of you, LOO THER.

The class, with unbridled enthusiasm, responds. There is no "th" in the whole melee. Miss Mather, with some effort, restores order.

MISS MATHER

Here, then, let's try this. I will show you how the sound is made, the "th" sound. You must place the tongue against the upper front teeth, like so, and vocalize . . . release the breath.

She demonstrates; "thuh, thuh, thuh, thuh." Again the class comes up with every thing but "thuh." Miss Mather is exasperated, but then inspiration strikes.

MISS MATHER

You need to see exactly what I am doing with my tongue and teeth. SEE!

She emphatically removes her dentures from her mouth and jabs her finger against the teeth. There is a moment of shocked silence on the part of the boys, then titters, then thunderous delight.

Interior. Boys' dormitory. Night. The secret society is meeting. Again there is the circle around the hooded light. We recognize the faces, but for the first time Thorpe is present. After a long moment of silence:

PLENTY HORSES

I dreamed. It was powerful. Clouds were rolling around me. I could not see. Then there was a voice, a voice like an echo, not loud, but somehow clear. It said that I must go home, and that I must take Grass home. The time has come. That is what I dreamed.

It is not like him to speak up, and we have the sense that the dream is indeed powerful and portentous. And we see this registered in the faces of the others.

Joseph Tso-odle we have not heard from before, but he has been a face in the crowd. In the almost hypnotic setting of the meeting, he is moved to speak.

JOSEPH TSO-ODLE

Sometimes I dream of my grandfather. He told me stories. He was crippled. He had been shot by soldiers at the Washita. He told me about that, how many of his family died there, and he cried when he told it. The soldiers charged into the village at daylight and shot him and everyone they could find. Some of our people ran and tried to hide, but most of them were run down and killed. It was winter and cold, and there was blood everywhere on the ice and in the water, and there were dead and wounded Indians on the ground. My grandfather's leg was torn; I guess the soldiers thought he would die. One of the soldiers said to him, "We will kill you all. We will pursue you, and we will kill your horses."

His voice has broken, and he drops his head; his shoulders shake with weeping.

Close on: Thorpe. He stares at Tso-odle with narrow eyes. We cannot read what he is thinking, but his gaze is intense.

Exterior. Carlisle green. Day. Luther, Ernest, and a group of boy students gather around excitedly as a wagon arrives, loaded with crates of gleaming band instruments, the donation of Philadelphia chocolate baron Walter Baker. Mrs. Baker supervises the delivery. Mason assists her. The Indians have never seen such a gleaming horde. A photographer is on hand. Mrs. Baker beams with philanthropic enthusiasm as she tries her best to converse with the boys, who squeal with delight among themselves in several languages, including English. Mason looks on, wondering why there is such excitement over a wagonload of band instruments. Ernest, who is weak and wheezing, seems almost to gather strength at the sight of these beautiful, shining instruments. He imagines they are exotic treasures, perhaps the latest weapons of war. But when he discovers the drums, he is nearly transported with awe and admiration. Even Plenty Horses, whose reticence is so practiced, cannot help being seduced by the drums. Pollack Spotted Tail tries to wrest the drumsticks away from Plenty Horses, but the older boy pushes him away. Max Spotted Tail hands his younger brother a French horn, with which Pollack wrestles in delight. Luther takes up a cornet. It is love at first sight.

LUTHER

(*voiceover*) Though we didn't know it, one of the things we missed most was music. It was a hunger in us in the early days. We had always had music in the camps, music and dancing. When the band instruments came to Carlisle, we knew suddenly that we had been starved for music. We formed a band, one that became nationally recognized. We marched in Washington and Philadelphia. We marched across the Brooklyn Bridge. When we could play together as a band, high-stepping and swinging the instruments in perfect unison, in harmony, we were in our element. We were at home.

Dissolve to: Historical photo of marching band.

Carlisle Indian School Band, with director Claude Stauffer (*standing, front*).
Courtesy of Cumberland County Historical Society, Carlisle, Pennsylvania.

Dissolve to: Football field, West Point, Day. It is halftime. Luther's son has gone down to run on the field with his cornet. He darts in and out, as if he is dodging tacklers. Luther and Pratt sit in the stands. Luther calls to his son to come back, shouting to him in Lakota.

Close on: Luther and Pratt.

PRATT

>   I am surprised that you speak to your son in Lakota.

LUTHER

>   (*jocular*) Oh, Captain. We spoke our languages in the old days at the school, too. You just didn't know about it. (*Pratt doesn't smile.*)

PRATT

>   If I had known, you might be better off.

LUTHER

>   If you had known, I might never have had my son, that fine boy running there on the field. I courted his mother in Lakota.

PRATT

>   I tried to do the right thing, you know. I tried to make proper citizens of you, all of you.

LUTHER

>   You were a force in our lives, Captain, night and day.

PRATT

>   Was I too stern a taskmaster, Luther, a thorn in your side?

LUTHER

>   Sometimes. But you were fair . . . most of the time.

PRATT

>   We have walked a long path, you and I.

LUTHER

>   Remember when you gave us tools? I thought they must be weapons, instruments of torture.

PRATT

>   Yes—and wonder of wonders—you became a pretty good carpenter. Imagine.

LUTHER

>   Imagine that.

PRATT

>   It *was* a transformation, you must admit. When you first came to the school, you were . . .

LUTHER

Not a carpenter, that's for sure.

PRATT

You were . . .

LUTHER

A savage?

PRATT

You were . . . unschooled, unsophisticated. You were an Indian.

LUTHER

I still am. Imagine.

A beat, in which Pratt seems at a loss.

PRATT

Why, you were the leader of the band!

LUTHER

Oh, what a band we were. You gave me my first cornet. Now my son plays it better than I do.

Luther's son joins them, blows "Charge" on his cornet.

Interior. Pratt's house, Carlisle. Night. A dinner, in the Pratt home. There are four guests—Etahdleuh, Lame, Luther, and Maggie Stands Looking. Lame is Etahdleuh's intended. She has come very recently from the Kiowa reservation. Luther and Maggie have been keeping company. Pratt presides over the meal; Anna is enjoying the chance to be a gracious hostess.

PRATT

Well, just look at this table: good food, good company. Mrs. Pratt and I are so glad you are with us. Lame, I want to welcome you. Etahdleuh has told us a great deal about you, all of it glowing, of course.

ANNA

Yes, yes, indeed. Dear Lame, I know that you must miss your family in the Territory. You are a long way from home, I know, but, dear, we so want you to feel at home here, as these other young people do. If there is anything you need, anything at all . . . please just ask. Our home is your home.

PRATT

> You have only to ask. This school is yours, you know. It belongs to you. Yes, indeed. It was founded for you, for all Indian people. Why, it is more yours than ours.

LAME

> (*softly, shyly*) Thank you, Captain Pratt, Mrs. Pratt.

ETAHDLEUH

> (*slowly, distinctly, as if reciting a memorized speech*) Captain, Mrs. Pratt, we are very happy to be here. We are grateful for your hos . . . your hospitality. Thank you.

LAME

> Yes, it is very good of you to have us in your home.

ANNA

> (*to Lame*) Your English is very good. Where did you learn to speak it?

LAME

> I learned from the Baptist missionaries. There is a church at Rainy Mountain.

PRATT

> Ah, Baptists, hey? We might have known. They are an aggressive lot.

ANNA

> Captain Pratt means, they have a wonderful . . . enthusiasm, a zeal for accomplishing the Lord's work.

PRATT

> Precisely what I meant.

LAME

> Yes, ma'am, yes, sir.

PRATT

> Luther, Maggie, what about the Rosebud, Pine Ridge. Are there missionaries there as well?

LUTHER

> I hear that there are Catholic priests now, a mission near one of the agencies.

Pratt seems somewhat irritated to hear this. Anna interjects a change of subject.

ANNA

> Maggie, dear, I hear that you are becoming quite an artist. Your instructor speaks so well of you.

MAGGIE

> We are learning to paint with watercolors. Mr. Marks is a very good teacher.

PRATT

> You know, on the subject of art. Indian people seem to have a remarkable facility for drawing and painting. Etahdleuh has drawn wonderful pictures. Several of the Indians at Fort Marion drew in ledger books. With colored pencils. I have saved their work. It is extraordinary.

LUTHER

> I suppose it was a way of overcoming homesickness.

ETAHDLEUH

> (almost inaudibly) Yes, yes.

Pratt regards them both for a long moment.

PRATT

> Well, to the real reason for this gathering! There is something I want to say. I have been thinking about it for some time—we, Mrs. Pratt and I. (There is a long, suspenseful moment.) I have decided . . . that I would like to adopt you, Etahdleuh, into my family.

Etahdleuh is silent for several beats. It is an awkward pause. He is probably not surprised; he has suspected this possibility for some time. As usual, we can read nothing in his face.

ETAHDLEUH

> Captain . . . Captain Pratt . . .

PRATT

> As a son, my son.

Lame glances suddenly at Etahdleuh.

ANNA

> And you, too, Lame! Now that the two of you are engaged to be

married, you, too, of course! You will be a daughter to us, and
we will call you Laura—if you don't mind—after my grandmother. It will be your new name, your Carlisle name!

*Lame manages a smile, but beneath her smile is a reserve that all but shows
through.*

PRATT

God bless us! This night we dine in celebration, in joy and
triumph! Everything I hoped for is coming to pass! Now, a
toast!

*He has poured wine for all. He raises his glass. The guests raise their glasses, but
they do not drink; they touch the glasses to their lips.*

ETAHDLEUH

Coming . . . to pass.

*Anna, Luther, and Maggie repeat "coming to pass." Lame looks into her wine
as if it is an oracle.*

*Exterior. Carlisle green. Night. Etahdleuh, Lame, Luther, and Maggie walk
back to the dormitories after dinner.*

LAME

You did not tell them.

ETAHDLEUH

No.

LUTHER

Tell them . . . who?—what?

LAME

We, Etahdleuh and I, are going home. We are going to be
missionaries to our people. We are going to lead our people on
the Jesus road.

*Close on: Luther is struck dumb. Like the others, he has come to depend on
Etahdleuh in many ways, most importantly as the one person who has protected the Indian heritage at Carlisle. Not only is Etahdleuh going to abandon
the children; he is going to espouse Christianity as a missionary. Luther can
only feel somehow betrayed, and we see this in his expression.*

LUTHER

> (*voiceover*) It seemed a troublesome time. The course of the Carlisle Indian Industrial School was changing; things were coming apart. I spent hours alone, walking in the woods, standing in the night and gazing at the stars. My best friend Ernest White Thunder was growing weaker every day. Plenty Horses and Etahdleuh were going to leave. The motion of the world seemed to have slowed almost to a standstill. I became despondent. Sometimes all I could do was play my horn.

The plaintive notes of his cornet.

Interior. Conference room adjoining Pratt's office, Carlisle. Day.
Close on: Pratt is seated at his desk, resplendent beside an American flag.

PRATT

> This court is now in session.

There is a pregnant pause in which Pratt surveys the room gravely. This is another opportunity for drama, and he savors it.

Pratt's point of view. The room has been converted into a courtroom. There are a number of boys in chairs. In the forefront are two men at desks, Stallworth and Kingsly. There is an air of apprehension, gravity.
Angle on:

PRATT

> We shall observe proper military procedures. One of our Carlisle students, Mr. Pollack Spotted Tail, is accused of behavior inappropriate to his station, to the Carlisle Indian Industrial School, and indeed to the society at large. This court is convened so that he may have the chance to face his accusers, to defend himself, and to be judged fairly by his peers in the light of testimony and evidence forthcoming. Will the accused please stand. (*to Pollack*) Please state your name.

POLLACK

> I am Spotted Tail's son.

PRATT

> Just *your* name.

POLLACK

 Spotted Tail.

PRATT

 (*showing anger*) You will tell me your name, Mister. When you entered Carlisle, you were given a first name, a Christian name. What is your name?

POLLACK

 Pollack . . . Spotted Tail.

PRATT

 Pollack Spotted Tail, SIR.

POLLACK

 Pollack Spotted Tail, SIR.

PRATT

 Do you solemnly swear to tell the truth here, so help you God?

POLLACK

 Yes.

PRATT

 Say, "I do."

POLLACK

 I do.

PRATT

 Be seated. (*Pratt stands tall, addresses the court.*) This court has appointed Mr. Stallworth, teacher and disciplinarian, to serve as the prosecuting officer, and Lieutenant Kingsly of the United States Army to represent the defense. (*pause*)

 May I remind those of you students who sit in judgment here today that your decision in the matter at hand will be considered final and binding. Mr. Stallworth . . .

Stallworth stands, looks over his glasses.

STALLWORTH

 Thank you, sir. I would like to call Mr. Stacy Matlock to the stand.

Stacy Matlock rises reluctantly and steps forward and takes the oath. He sits in a chair provided.

STALLWORTH

> Now, Mr. Matlock, will you please tell the court, as precisely as you can, what happened on the afternoon of August 20 last, to the best of your recollection?

STACY MATLOCK

> There was a fight. Pollack stabbed Plenty Horses.

STALLWORTH

> We will need you to elaborate, Mr. Matlock. I will ask you specific questions. Where did this occurrence take place?

STACY MATLOCK

> In the metal shop . . . blacksmith shop.

STALLWORTH

> What were you doing there?

STACY MATLOCK

> There was a class; we were in class.

STALLWORTH

> Mr. Arnold was teaching a class there, wasn't he? A class in metalwork.

STACY MATLOCK

> Yes.

STALLWORTH

> And you, and Mr. Spotted Tail—Mr. Pollack Spotted Tail, that is—and Mr. Plenty Horses were there, as members of the class?

STACY MATLOCK

> Yes.

STALLWORTH

> And during class, what happened?

STACY MATLOCK

> Like I said, Pollack stabbed Plenty Horses.

STALLWORTH

> Where in the shop did this happen, exactly?

STACY MATLOCK

> I don't know, at one of the tables.

STALLWORTH

> Were Mr. Spotted Tail and Mr. Plenty Horses working together?

STACY MATLOCK

> Yes . . . no. They were near each other.

STALLWORTH

> And then what happened?

STACY MATLOCK

They got into a fight. Pollack stabbed Plenty Horses.

STALLWORTH

What was the fight about, what caused it?

STACY MATLOCK

I don't know. They don't like each other.

Stallworth takes from the top of his desk piece of metal, a chisel, and shows it to Stacy Matlock.

STALLWORTH

Is this the instrument with which Mr. Spotted Tail stabbed Mr. Plenty Horses?

STACY MATLOCK

Yes.

STALLWORTH

And what was the extent of the injury, Mr. Matlock?

STACY MATLOCK

What?

STALLWORTH

How seriously was Mr. Plenty Horses wounded?

STACY MATLOCK

Not bad . . . just a little blood.

STALLWORTH

Thank you. *(to Pratt)* That's all I have for this witness, sir.

PRATT

Thank you. Lieutenant Kingsly?

KINGSLY

I have no questions for this witness, sir.

Later in the day, same setting. Lieutenant Kingsly is questioning Max Spotted Tail.

KINGSLY

You are Pollack Spotted Tail's older brother, is that right?

MAX

Yes, sir.

KINGSLY

You heard Mr. Matlock's testimony earlier today. Would you say that his account of what happened is accurate?

MAX

Stacy didn't tell everything.

KINGSLY

What didn't he tell, Mr. Spotted Tail? What did he leave out?

MAX

Plenty Horses picks on my brother. All the time. Plenty Horses is older. He shouldn't do it. He made Pollack mad, that's all.

KINGSLY

You are saying that Mr. Plenty Horses goaded your brother into a fight, is that right?

MAX

Yes, sir.

KINGSLY

In your view, Mr. Plenty Horses brought the incident on himself, is that right? He is responsible for what happened?

MAX

Yes, sir.

KINGSLY

(to Pratt) That's all I have, sir.

PRATT

Your witness, Mr. Stallworth.

Stallworth gets up and walks slowly to Max. He is sure of himself, having heard the testimony.

STALLWORTH

Just one or two questions, Mr. Spotted Tail, if you please. Did you see your brother, Mr. Pollard Spotted Tail, deliberately attack Mr. Plenty Horses with the metal tool in evidence, and did he inflict a wound? Yes or no?

MAX

(softly, after a long pause) Yes.

STALLWORTH

Did Mr. Plenty Horses have a weapon, or any object with which to defend himself?

Max barely shakes his head.

STALLWORTH
   Please answer so that the court can hear you, Mr. Spotted Tail.
MAX
   No.
STALLWORTH
   (to Pratt) No further questions, Captain Pratt.

Later. Same setting. Pollack Spotted Tail stands before Pratt.

PRATT
   Pollack Spotted Tail. You have been found guilty, by a body of
   your peers, of the charges brought against you. I hereby sen-
   tence you to one month in the guardhouse. This court is ad-
   journed.

*Dissolve to: Interior. Boys' dormitory. Night. The boys are distressed by the
outcome of the trial. Max, especially, is distraught. He has tried to be fair, and
he has told the truth, but he nonetheless feels that he has betrayed a member of
his tribe and his family. Luther understands and tries to comfort Max, but he
too feels caught up in a cultural crossfire. Plenty Horses sits brooding in a
corner, staring into the night.*

*Dissolve to: The Pratt house, living room. Night. It is late. Pratt is alone. He
has fallen asleep in his easy chair. He twitches, apparently dreaming. A figure
in silhouette appears in the doorway. He looks up, blinking.*

PRATT
   Who's there? . . . you? *(It is Grass. She stares at him through her
   glasses. The light is such that the large lenses reflect it. Otherwise she is in
   shadow, dimly visible.)* What is it? What do you want? *(He is shaken.)*
GRASS
   I have come to forgive you.
PRATT
   Forgive? Me? What are you . . . talking about?
GRASS
   You dishonored my death. You threw me away. You buried me
   without a name, as if I had not lived. It was shameful.

Pratt is in a cold sweat. He does not know if he is awake or if he is dreaming.

PRATT

No, no. I . . . I don't know . . . what you're talking about.

GRASS

It doesn't matter. I have earned my death. I am going home. I forgive you.

Pratt blinks. This is beyond him. His expression goes from fear to anger.

PRATT

You forgive me? Why, why, how dare you! I don't want your forgiveness. I have done nothing to be forgiven! How dare you?

She is perfectly calm, serene.

GRASS

The warriors and the chiefs have brought medicine for me. And they will soon bring medicine for you. Do not be afraid. Be at peace. They will bring you sage and sweetgrass. When they come, and you see them, how beautiful and fierce they are in their war paint, you will grow peaceful, won't you? When you hear their cries and their honor songs, when you hear the beating of their horses' hooves, you will be peaceful, won't you? And when they touch you and let you go, you will be peaceful, won't you? I forgive you. *Aiyeee! (She is gone.)*

Dissolve to: Luther plays taps, weeping, over the grave of Ernest White Thunder.

Exterior. Lawn of Pratt house. Day. Pratt and General Hancock sit in chairs conversing over tea.

PRATT

At Fort Marion we gave them instruction, but more than that, we gave them responsibility and a wholesome environment and Christian ethics . . . and trust. Yes sir, we gave them our trust.

GENERAL HANCOCK

I understand. But it was a trade-off, wasn't it? You took some-

thing away from them, too—their language, their freedom,
their culture. . . .

PRATT

Make no mistake, General. We had no choice. They faced extinction.

GENERAL HANCOCK

And your students here, do they face extinction as well?

PRATT

They forestall extinction, at least. You know, General, these
students serve their own people by example. And they serve us
as well.

GENERAL HANCOCK

How so? What do you mean?

PRATT

Don't you see, they are a deterrent to further hostilities in the
West.

GENERAL HANCOCK

You mean, Richard, they are hostages?

Pratt is unbalanced by the question. He stammers:

PRATT

No, well, no. I certainly wouldn't use that word, General. You,
you know what I mean.

Dissolve to: Exterior. Woods. Day. Etahdleuh walks, looking for Luther. He
finds him in the cemetery. Etahdleuh carries a bundle in his hands. He holds it
out to Luther.

ETAHDLEUH

I would like to give you this.

LUTHER

What is it?

ETAHDLEUH

You remember the night the Captain came into the dorm and
found you talking after hours? He discovered Ernest's medicine pouch and ordered me to collect all such things and dis-
pose of them.

LUTHER

I remember.

ETAHDLEUH

Those things are here in this bundle.

LUTHER

What do you want me to do with them?

ETAHDLEUH

I have thought hard on it, for a long time. These things are not
of this world. They are sacred objects that belong to our people. They are powerful and full of spirit. I could not destroy
them or throw them away. They are what we have of our past.
Lame and I are going home, but we are going as Christians and
missionaries. These things no longer truly belong to me, to us.
They belong to you. I know your heart. You are meant to be a
keeper of medicine bundles, a holy man, a chief. I know that,
son of Standing Bear.

They fall into a long, hard embrace.

Interior. Boys' dormitory. Night. A meeting of the secret society.

LUTHER

Great Mystery, we make an offering of our words. Hear us.
We pray to you
with our living breath
with our going forth
with our standing fast
with our dreaming
in the words of our ancestors in the proper way
Aho

*Joseph Tso-odle has made a drum from a kettle and a patch of leather. He beats
the drum very lowly, and the others begin to sing softly. It is a farewell song in
Plenty Horses' honor.*

LUTHER

We pray that our words go with Plenty Horses, that he goes in
safety, with good feelings and a good heart, that he will give

our hearts to all those at home, to our families, to the old people, to the children we love but have not seen, our little brothers and sisters.

(Superimposed on this scene: Plenty Horses looks out from train window, sees remembered landmarks.) We pray that one day we will follow in his steps, that we will return to our homes and our people, to the center of our ancient world, to the place of origin.

(Plenty Horses walks among the Lakota houses and camps. He carries a tattered suitcase.) We pray that we will follow in his steps, that we will be his shadow, that we will be the honor song on his breath.

(Plenty Horses stops before the door of a broken-down house, opens the suitcase and removes Grass's glasses and doll. A woman opens the door, and he hands her these things. They say nothing, but there is a long moment between them. Then she nods and closes the door. Plenty Horses moves on.) We pray that our brother will be a warrior.

Exterior. No Water, near Pine Ridge. Day. It is a few days after the massacre at Wounded Knee. Cavalry Lieutenant Edward Casey, with five Cheyenne scouts, rides under a flag of truce. He is met by several Lakota men on horseback, Plenty Horses among them. They talk for a time, gesturing now and then in sign language. We cannot hear what is being said. Then Casey and the scouts ride on. The Lakota men watch them, then Plenty Horses raises a rifle and shoots Casey in the back, killing him instantly. His body slumps and falls in the snow.

Dissolve to: Exterior. Thanksgiving Day, Carlisle. Day. There is a large gathering on the green. It is a day for Pratt to show off the school. Many important people have been invited, including several Lakota chiefs, Spotted Tail and Standing Bear among them. Some of the younger children, dressed as pilgrims, are presenting a play. Mason, dressed as a huge turkey and playing to the crowd, draws loud laughter. Then, from the bandstand:
Close on: Pratt and Spotted Tail.

PRATT

And now, ladies and gentlemen, students, and friends of Carlisle, it is my honor to present to you the great chief Spotted Tail of the Lakota nation!

Spotted Tail looks over the crowd.

SPOTTED TAIL

(*through Tackett*) You ask me to speak. I will give you my words. I will speak from my heart. Hear me! I am sad, and I am angry.

Pratt senses in the chief's voice that things are going wrong here. He looks around nervously, as if for help.

SPOTTED TAIL

This white man, Captain Pratt, has lied to me and to my people. I allowed him to take my children. He said that he would teach them good things, that they would return to help us. Now I come here to see my children and to see what is being done to them. I do not like what I see. I see Lakota boys wear the uniforms of the long knives. I see that their hair has been stolen, their names have been stolen, their language has been stolen.

Pratt is nearly wild in his eyes. He interrupts:

PRATT

Chief, there is a misunderstanding. . . . If you do me the courtesy . . .

SPOTTED TAIL

NO! I speak! You hear me! You lock my little son in stone house. NO GOOD! NO MORE! I will take my children home! Now!

PRATT

Please listen to me! Your eldest son Max was a member of the tribunal that pun . . . that disciplined your son Pollack. You understand that discipline. . . . My God, are my words being translated?

SPOTTED TAIL

You make brother enemy to brother, son enemy to father. I will take my children home. Now.

Several people, including journalists and General Hancock, try to speak to Pratt, but he brushes past them blindly in a daze.

LUTHER

(voiceover) Those that I had loved most at the school were gone. The news that Plenty Horses had killed an American soldier came to me many days afterwards. I was shocked and sad beyond the telling. I hid from everyone, even Maggie. I felt that I, too, had to leave. But I could not yet go home. All that had taken place had made me very unhealthy in my mind. Maggie drew away from me, and I could not blame her. Etahdleuh and Lame were gone. Plenty Horses was gone. Ernest was dead. I told Captain Pratt that I wanted to take part in the Outing Program, to be placed in a job away from the school. He found a place for me in Wanamaker's Department Store in Philadelphia. I worked there for a time, but it did not satisfy me. Then one day, as I was walking from work I saw something that was completely unexpected: I saw that the West had come to Philadelphia.

Exterior. Philadelphia street. Day. Luther's attention is caught by a huge sign plastered on the wall of a building. On it are the faces of Buffalo Bill and Sitting Bull, Annie Oakley, and Geronimo. He is transfixed and reads aloud, "BUFFALO BILL'S WILD WEST SHOW! ONE WEEK ONLY. PHILADELPHIA FAIRGROUNDS. COME ONE, COME ALL!"

Interior. Tent, Wild West Show. Night. It is after the performance. Luther has gained entrance into Sitting Bull's dressing tent. The two speak in Lakota, with subtitles.

SITTING BULL

Yes, certainly I know your father.

LUTHER

Perhaps we are related, you and I.

SITTING BULL

(smiling) All Lakota are related.

LUTHER

I am excited, honored to meet you.

SITTING BULL

Because I am a famous actor?

LUTHER

No, no. Because you are a famous chief.

SITTING BULL

I am chief of the arena. I kill Custer every night and twice on Sunday.

LUTHER

I want to ask you why. Respectfully. Why did you join the Wild West Show?

SITTING BULL

Let me answer you as truthfully as I can. I am not sure. It is better than sitting hungry and cold on the reservation, with nowhere to go and nothing to do but remember old times. It is exciting, the color and smoke. I travel to places that I never knew existed. Everywhere I go people look up to me. I am the dream of children come true. Most of all, I think, it is a way for me to return to the world I knew before the white man came. It allows me to imagine what I used to be. And, you see, it is almost enough. I am almost my own dream come true.

LUTHER

Do you think I could join the show?

SITTING BULL

You would have to get a wig, and you would have to change out of those civilized clothes. Oh, and you would have to paint your face.

LUTHER

What color?

SITTING BULL

Fierce.

Exterior. Another tent. Wild West Show. Day. Luther is getting dressed, made up for the performance. Pratt enters. Luther shows little, if any, surprise. There are uneasy greetings.

LUTHER

I guess I knew that you would find me.

PRATT

At Wanamaker's they told me you were here.

LUTHER

I am an Apache tonight.

PRATT

Well, Luther, I must say that I find it ironic—and disappointing as well—to see you dressing up like an Indian.

LUTHER

The irony is that I am an Indian.

PRATT

You were, when I found you.

LUTHER

You taught me to dress like a white man. But I did not therefore become a white man.

PRATT

(*sighs*) Apparently not.

LUTHER

In some way, I believe, I will always be my father's son.

PRATT

As you know, it is my contention that your father grew up in a world that no longer exists. This . . . this spectacle, "The Wild West Show," is nothing but a crude imitation of that former world, the West as it was for your father. I know. I remember how it was out there before you were born. I was a young soldier facing real enemies, not actors, doing my duty for my country, not performing for a crowd of hooting spectators. And your father was the same—by and large. I could look him in the eye. I could respect him.

LUTHER

(*anger growing up in him*) You can look me in the eye, and I will not blink. And I will have your respect. I demand it. Yes, this is make-believe, but so was Carlisle. I had to pretend there that I was not who I am. I am tired of that pretension. This one is better, at least for me, for the time being. It may well be more honest. Bright lights, greasepaint, buffalo that live in cages, trained prairie dogs. But at least we are Indians in the arena, men who under their poster paint and cotton buckskins are Indians, real Indians. And I am one of them. Do you know that when I return to the Lakota, I will be a real chief?

Pratt is subdued by this, sorry that he has angered a friend and former student.

PRATT

Yes, I see that you . . . you are right, of course. I spoke out of turn.

LUTHER

It's all right. So did I.

PRATT

I did not come to scold you or spy upon you. There is something I must tell you. Etahdleuh . . .

LUTHER

Ah, how is he? I miss him. I hear that Lame has borne him a son, named after you, I believe. You must be proud.

PRATT

(*painfully*) Etahdleuh is . . . Etahdleuh is dead. Apparently he had been sick for a time. I don't know the details. Laura . . . Lame . . . telegraphed.

(*Luther cannot speak.*)

He was with me from the time of Fort Marion—from the beginning. Like you, Luther, he was my darling.

Luther slumps to the dressing table. A pot of red paint drops to the floor and spreads, forming a small pool.

IV

Exterior. Football field, West Point. Late afternoon. The game is over. The scoreboard shows: CARLISLE 27. ARMY 6. The players of both teams—dirty, bloody, exhausted—mingle, shaking hands on their way to the locker rooms. Dwight Eisenhower, limping badly, makes a great effort to intercept Jim Thorpe. He extends his hand and seems to want to say something but doesn't. His silence is pure tribute. Thorpe takes his hand, regards him for a moment.

THORPE

We will not pursue you, and we will not kill your horses.

Close on: A montage of photographs showing the Carlisle football team of 1912. There are photographs of Thorpe in athletic poses, some of the game, showing Thorpe in action.

Players on the 1912 Carlisle football team. *Front row (l. to r.):* Charles William, Peter Calac, Elmer Busch, Joseph Bergie, William Garlow, Joe Guyon, Roy Large. *Back row:* Alex Arcasa, Stancil "Possum" Powell, Gus Welch, Jim Thorpe. Courtesy of Cumberland County Historical Society, Carlisle, Pennsylvania.

Jim Thorpe kicking the football for Carlisle Indian School in the game against Toronto, October 28, 1912. Courtesy of Cumberland County Historical Society, Carlisle, Pennsylvania.

Interior. Hotel lobby, New York City. Night. Pratt and Luther have come here after the game to visit and reminisce before going their separate ways. Luther's son has fallen asleep in a nearby chair. A waiter brings them tea.

PRATT

> Remember . . . Well, you remember.

LUTHER

> I remember it all, Captain. Everything. I do remember. I remember, as a little boy on the train, I saw the moon in the window where I sat. And then, a few moments later, I saw the moon in the window on the other side of the train. It seemed to me that the moon had flown across the sky. I was frightened.

PRATT

> Isn't that funny? It happens to me, too. There are many turns in the road, isn't that so? You had been turned around without knowing it. You were disoriented.

LUTHER

> There was more to it than that, I think. The moon in two windows. It is a strange thing somehow, an unnatural thing. What you Christians call a miracle.

PRATT

> What is natural, I wonder. The natural world you lived in was hopeless. The miracle was that you escaped it. I like to think that I had something to do with bringing about that miracle. With the help of others—and with God's help above all—I saved those I could.

LUTHER

> Richard, have you been to the cemetery?

PRATT

> What? The cemetery?

LUTHER

> At the school. The graves of the children. Many people go there now. They bring flowers and ribbons—sometimes tobacco and cornmeal, pollen. Have you gone there?

PRATT

> You have to understand that the young people who died there were beyond help. They were dying before they left the camps. We must think of the ones who didn't die, the many hundreds

who lived. They are healthy, happy human beings. And they produce healthy, happy children of their own. They are well-adjusted Americans. They are . . .

LUTHER

Civilized.

PRATT

Yes, indeed, civilized. *(Pratt slowly gets to his feet. He has grown feeble with age.)* I must go, Luther. Shake my hand. It was wonderful to see you again.

Luther stands and takes his hand.

Good night, Captain Pratt, and goodbye.

Dissolve to: Exterior. Arlington National Cemetery. Day. Luther stands at Pratt's grave. On the simple headstone are the words:

RICHARD HENRY PRATT

ERECTED IN LOVING MEMORY

BY HIS STUDENTS AND OTHER INDIANS

Exterior. Carlisle Cemetery. Day. Luther and Stone walk among the headstones. They are the only ones there.

LUTHER

(voiceover) The Indian Industrial School at Carlisle was a kind of laboratory in which our hearts were tested. We were all shaped by that experience. Some of us were destroyed, and some were made stronger. I believe that; I know that to be true. Captain Pratt, and others after him, came for the children and took them away. For every one of them, for every single child, it was a passage into darkness. It was a kind of quest, not a quest for glory, but a quest for survival. They were all brave; they did a brave thing. Those who died on the journey were especially brave, and their bravery is signed here in stone. Theirs is the sacrifice that makes sacred this ground. But they were all brave, those who lived and those who died; all were marked by Carlisle. We were children who ventured into the unknown. And if again my father told me to go away from my Indian

home into an alien world that I could not have imagined, I would do it. I would go, as all of us did, with all the love and courage in my heart. I would do a brave thing.

Father and son go out of the cemetery and walk on the grounds of the school. As they approach Indian Field, Stone pulls his father's hand, and they stop and stand still. Stone points to two figures, distant on the field, a man and a child. The man takes the child by both hands and swings her round and round.

END OF PLAY

The Carlisle Indian School Cemetery in the 1930s. Copy of a small snapshot, courtesy of Cumberland County Historical Society, Carlisle, Pennsylvania.